He Gets The Last Word

He Gets The Last Word

~

Consider Him one Word at a time.
Inspiring devotionals to fill your
mind before you say Good Night!

By
Wendy Miller

O'Neill, J. (1971, October 6) The True Story of The Patton Prayer. Retrieved from http://www.pattonhq.com/prayer.html

ISBN-13: 9780998397405
ISBN-10: 0998397407

Blessed Acknowledgements!

He Gets The Last Word is an accumulation of personal reflections that have been written over the course of five years. I would like my readers to know the journey leading to the completion of this devotional includes the many roles that I have played as a woman. I have written as a sister, daughter, wife, mother, friend, ministry leader, and someone who has had to overcome the hurdles of great unexpected loss of relationships in the last two years. I hope to impart my chosen outlook on life, which is to trust and surrender to a loving Savior who will never abandon anyone who seeks Him through the Word.

Firstly, I would like to praise my Lord and Savior, Jesus Christ, and I give thanks to His Holy Spirit in helping me to complete this project. I want to acknowledge all of my friends and family who have been the inspiration to so many of my reflections. A special measure of love and gratefulness to Kylie Hughes, Skylar Hughes, Dr. John & Joan Miller, and Kavi Mehta for their loyalty and strength through this journey called life.

My heartfelt gratitude to all my sisters in Christ who have cheered me on. Sheryl Murdock, Diedre Hayes, Laura Burdge, Heidi Embleton, Wailani O'Herlihy, Lisa Houge, Mimi Aiello, Brooke Turpin, Alicia Harris, Michele del Toro, Karen Waldron, Jaclyn Kornreich, Kimberly Cowan, Brenda Epperson, Cindy Bond, Robin Hanley and Deborah Flora. I appreciate the loyalty and patience of the incredible men in my life who have supported me during this journey; John Embleton, Bud Murdock, Chad Hayes, Tom Turpin, and Doug Burdge. I would also like to give a special praise to Rabbi Jason Sobel and Bodie Thoene for all the divinely appointed phone calls, and persistent prayers that helped to make this project happen. I still continue to place my hope in Heaven's cisterns of prayers one day tipping over and being lovingly poured out over the entire Hughes and Gustavson families. I pray for His glory, redemption, restoration, and transformation for everyone within the body of Christ, and an extra measure for all my loved ones!

So, praise God, go Jesus, and I humbly and graciously thank His Holy Spirit who held my hand, taught, revealed, and inspired each devotional. My prayer is that each reader's life will be touched by the power of His scriptures, as *He Gets The Last Word*!

Blessings,
Wendy

"In the beginning the Word already existed.
The Word was with God, and the Word was God."

John 1:1 NLT

Table of Contents

"Angry"

"Why are you so angry? The Lord asked Cain. Why do you look so dejected?"

Genesis 4:6 NLT

Do you just feel angry sometimes? Are there people, situations, injustices, disappointments, frustrations, insecurities, and hurtful rejections that just make your blood boil? If so, then you are not alone. Anger is mentioned in Genesis, the first book, and the fourth chapter of the Bible. Anger has been here since the beginning. It is a normal human emotion that even small babies experience. It is the secondary emotion behind painful emotions like the ones listed above. A healthful and scriptural way to deal with anger is something we should all seek.

This is particularly true for women, who have learned that "pitching a fit" or displaying anger is unacceptable, but have never learned how to let go of the negative emotions and heal. Instead women tend to vent to their friends about an "infraction" that made them upset, or just try to hold it together, while in reality they are steaming on the inside. Some women do not know how to let go of the anger and deal with the hurt. Instead, they will distance themselves from that which has offended them and just hang on to the upset feelings. Subconsciously, women will silently hold a grudge and un-forgiveness for years in their hearts. They will never truly deal with the emotional hurt behind the anger.

The feelings become suppressed. This can be dangerous and toxic not only to one's health, but also to one's psychological state of mind and spiritual peace.

> *"Why are you so angry? The Lord asked Cain, Why do you look so dejected? You will be accepted if you do what is right. But if you refuse to do what is right, then watch out! Sin is crouching at the door, eager to control you. But you must subdue it and be its master."*
>
> *Genesis 4:6-7 NLT*

So, what is the right way to deal with our anger? The Bible gives these thoughtful insights:

> *"And don't sin by letting anger control you. Don't let the sun go down while you are still angry, for anger gives a foothold to the devil...Get rid of all bitterness, rage, anger, harsh words, and slander, as well as all types of evil behavior. Instead, be kind to each other, tenderhearted, forgiving one another, just as God through Christ has forgiven you."*
>
> *Ephesians 4:26-32 NLT*

> *"But now is the time to get rid of anger, rage, malicious behavior, slander and dirty language... Make allowance for each other's faults, and forgive anyone who offends you. Remember, the Lord forgave you, so you must forgive others. Above all clothe yourselves with love, which binds us all together in perfect harmony. And let the peace that comes from Christ rule in your hearts..."*
>
> *Colossians 3:8-15 NLT*

"Don't sin by letting anger control you. Think about it
overnight and remain silent."

Psalm 4:4 NLT

"But I say, if you are even angry with someone, you are subject
to judgment! If you call someone an idiot, you are in danger of
being brought before the court. And if you curse someone, you
are in danger of the fires of Hell."

Matthew 5:22 NLT

God urges us to come to Him and lay our burdens, including anger and hurt, at the foot of the cross. When we confess our "anger" in prayer, then the Lord can enter our hearts and supernaturally heal the primary emotions behind the anger. Our prayer is an act of obedience, motivated by our confidence and faith in Christ, to let Him do the impossible. We cannot do the healing on our own. Healing comes through the Holy Spirit's presence ministering His love to us.

It is not unusual to cry during the process of praying. God's love opens the floodgates of your heart, and then His healing power overflows and cleanses our wounds. The living water washes away the hurt and offense in our lives, often illustrated in the form of our tears. The peace and healing is supernatural. It is God. The prayer may be through gritted teeth and the pure act of obedience. You may not feel anything or have no emotional response, but the healing will still come. Sometimes the healing is instant, but sometimes it takes more time and more prayer.

You may think that some circumstances are so horrendous, cruel, and unjust that the idea of not being angry anymore seems impossible. How does one overcome the pain of the betrayal or loss? We overcome through the power of our testimony by trusting in the promises of God. It is important to deal with the hurt behind the anger. Suppressed anger can begin to affect your mind, body, and spirit. God is asking us to let go of our anger. God is big enough, and strong enough, and compassionate enough to take on our anger. Jesus promises to heal the pain of our broken hearts, fears, and hate from a fragmented world if we will come to Him. The act of forgiveness is actually a blessing for us. Forgiveness does not always happen overnight. Forgiveness can be a process, but it will free oneself from destructive emotions and lead to a healthier you!

Remember that anger is a natural reaction to offense, but don't hang on to it. Let it go and deal with the hurt through prayer. Don't allow your peace, nor joy to be stolen by remaining angry. Keeping in mind that even God gets angry sometime.

"But you, O Lord, are a God of compassion and mercy, slow to get angry and filled with unfailing love and faithfulness."

Psalm 86:15, Psalm 103:8, Psalm 145:8, Exodus 34:6 NLT

Ask yourself:

1) What does anger emotionally and physically feel like?
2) How does anger give the devil a foothold in your life? What are the impacts on you?
3) What does scripture say we should do with our anger? Which scripture particularly resonates with you?
4) The Bible says we are to love our enemies as we love ourselves and to do unto others as you would have them do unto you. Why is it so hard to let go of the anger we have toward those who have offended us? What makes it so hard to forgive?
5) Close your eyes and make a mental list of those people in your life, circumstances etc. that make you angry. Now see if you can choose a word which reflects the emotion *behind* the anger. Visualize the circumstance or person and listen to these words: betrayal, injustice, abandonment, rejection, pain, frustration,

indifference, disloyalty, humiliation, discrimination, persecution, disrespect, unloved, hopelessness, overwhelming, isolation, misunderstanding, unresolved, ambiguous, blame, shame, and dangerous.

Pray: We pray, Lord Jesus, that You would do an exchange for our emotions. Help us…give us the courage to silently confess our anger and ask forgiveness for harboring rage in our hearts and minds. We, by faith, believe that as we forgive, You will remove those hurts. Help us to begin the process today which will lead to better health and peace of mind. We receive all that You want to do in us by the power of Your Holy Spirit, our Heavenly Counselor and Holy Comforter. We willingly exchange the anger and emotions that held us back from walking in love, forgiveness, and freedom. "For that which God has set free is free indeed!" In the Mighty name of Jesus….Amen.

"Army"

*"Listen, a noise on the mountains, like that of a great
multitude! Listen, an uproar among the kingdoms,
like nations massing together! The LORD Almighty
is mustering an army for war."*

Isaiah 13:4 NIV

THE TRUMPET SOUNDS and the army rushes into battle. This is a scene depicted again and again by Hollywood with the likes of cavalries, hordes of sword-bearing barbarians, horse-drawn Roman chariots, and even an army of blue alien *Avatars*. I wanted to share the insights of a famous WWII general, and how he sounded the trumpet before going into battle. The following is a reflection written by a chaplain who served under General Patton.

The True Story of the Patton Prayer

The incident of the now famous Patton Prayer commenced with a telephone call to the Third Army Chaplain on the morning of December 8, 1944.

"This is General Patton; do you have a good prayer for weather? We must do something about those rains if we are to win the war." My reply was that I know where to look for such a prayer, that I would locate, and report within the hour. Keeping his immediate objective in mind, I typed an original prayer and handed it to the General.

Almighty and most merciful Father, we humbly beseech Thee, of Thy great goodness, to restrain these immoderate rains with which we have had to contend. Grant us fair weather for Battle. Graciously hearken to us as soldiers who call upon Thee that, armed with Thy power, we may advance from victory to victory, and crush the oppression and wickedness of our enemies and establish Thy justice among men and nations. To each officer and soldier in the Third United States Army, I wish a Merry Christmas. I have full confidence in your courage, devotion to duty, and skill in battle. We march in our might to complete victory. May God's blessings rest upon each of you on this Christmas day.

-G.S. Patton, Jr, Lieutenant General, Commanding, Third United States Army.

General Patton read the prayer and said, "Very good. Chaplain, sit down for a moment; I want to talk to you about this business of prayer. Chaplain, how much praying is being done in the Third Army?"

I parried: "Does the General mean by chaplains, or by the men?"

"By everybody," he replied.

To this I countered: "I am afraid to admit it, but I do not believe that much praying is going on. When there is fighting, everyone prays, but now with this constant rain -- when things are quiet, dangerously quiet, men just sit and wait for things to happen. Prayer out here is difficult. I do not believe that much praying is being done."

Patton replied, "Chaplain, I am a strong believer in prayer. There are three ways that men get what they want: by planning, by working, and by praying. Any great military operation takes careful planning, or thinking. Then you must have well-trained troops to carry it out: that's working. But between the plan and the operation there is always an unknown. That unknown spells defeat or victory, success or failure. It is the reaction of the actions to the ordeal when it actually comes. Some people call that getting the breaks; I call it God. God has His part, or margin in everything, that's where prayer comes in."

"Is not My word like fire," declares the LORD, and like a
hammer that breaks a rock in pieces?"

Jeremiah 23:29 NIV

"Up to now, in the Third Army, God has been very good to us. We have never retreated; we have suffered no defeats, no famine, and no epidemics. This is because a lot of people back home are praying for us. But we have to pray for ourselves, too."

"We use God's mighty weapons, not worldly weapons,
to knock down the strongholds of human reasoning
and to destroy false arguments."

2 Corinthians 10:4 NLT

"We've got to get not only the chaplains, but every man in the Third Army to pray. We must ask God to stop these rains. These rains are that margin that holds defeat or victory. If we all pray it will be like plugging in on a current whose source is in Heaven. I believe that prayer completes that circuit. It is power." Patton concluded with the statement, "We must march together, all out for God. This Army needs the assurance and the faith that God is with us. I believe that we can overcome our circumstance and suffering through our ability to believe in prayer. With prayer, we cannot fail."

"...If God is for us, who can stand against us?"

Romans 8:31 NIV

9

On December 20, to the consternation of the Germans and the delight of the Americans, the battlefields had a turn-about in the rains, and the fogs ceased. For the better part of a week came bright clear skies and perfect flying weather. Our planes came over by tens, hundreds, and thousands. General Patton prayed for fair weather for Battle. He got it. It was late in January of 1945 when I saw the Army Commander again in the city of Luxembourg. He stood directly in front of me, smiled: "Well, Padre, our prayers worked. I knew they would." Then he cracked me on the side of my steel helmet with his riding crop. That was his way of saying, "Well done."

by Msgr. James H. O'Neill

In reflection of the recount above, it is obvious that prayer makes a difference. And one of the greatest military minds knew it. What kind of difference would an army of prayer warriors make in your life, in your church, and in your community? I hope all of us can gleam the wisdom of Patton and pray through the battles in our lives, and enlist others to pray in agreement with us.

"Again, truly I tell you that if two of you on earth agree about anything they ask for, it will be done for them by My Father in Heaven. For where two or three gather in my name, there am I with them."

Matthew 18:19-20 NIV

Ask Yourself:

1) Whom do you want to be part of your prayer army?
2) What are the first set of issues your prayer army should address?
3) Have you contacted your fellow warriors to enlist them in the battle? Do it now!

Pray: Lord, You have told us to 'pray without ceasing.' You also tell us that prayer changes things. You tell us to bear each other's burdens. Lord, sometimes when someone ask me to pray for them I have said yes, but not really followed through. Help me to change that, starting right now. Bring someone's needs to mind and let me pray for them immediately. Then help me to be accountable by contacting them and telling them what I have done and what I'm going to do. In the strength of Almighty Jesus....Amen.

"Battle"

---~---

*"Be strong and of good courage; do not be afraid, nor be
dismayed, for the Lord your God is with you wherever you go."*

Joshua 1:9 NKJV

THESE WORDS ARE throughout the Bible as words of encouragement for
whatever we are facing. It is during our times of battle that the Lord
wants us to remember that He is always with us. He is fighting alongside
us, and even battling in the heavens for us.

The Lord spoke these words to Joshua as Joshua took over the
place of Moses and led his people out of the wilderness. He chose
Joshua as His new leader because of his faithfulness and obedience. If we face our trials like Joshua, with hope and faith, then
God will honor that. When God spoke, Joshua listened and obeyed.
Joshua's obedience can serve us as a model. We must have courage
and consistent faith. The trials that we face can often feel like a test
with a passing or failing grade. The more faith that we have during the trial, the more we will be honored by God. It is easy during our trials to blame God, or be angry with Him and turn away.
Unfortunately, that is just what the enemy wants for us. He wants
us to be separated from the One who gives us the strength to get
through the battle.

"Not by might nor by power, but by my Spirit, says the Lord Almighty."

Zechariah 4:6 NIV

God is the Creator of the universe who yearns for us to know Him. Unlike us, God knows what will happen tomorrow, next week, next year, and even in the next decade. More importantly, He knows what will occur in our lives and can be there for us, if we've chosen to include Him. He tells us that He can be "our refuge and strength, an ever-present help in times of trouble." But we must make a sincere effort to seek Him. That doesn't mean that those who know God will escape difficult times because in life they are inevitable. But there is a peace and a strength that God's presence gives. If we go through trials while knowing God, we can react to them with a different perspective, and with a strength that is not our own. Our job is to fight and to remain steadfast in the promises of the Word. How we handle ourselves in the midst of the battle makes the difference. No problem has the capacity to be insurmountable to God. He is bigger than all the problems that can hit us, and we are not left alone to deal with them. We must claim the promise of God that says

"For I can do everything through Christ who give me strength."

Philippians 4:13 NLT

Fortunately, our battles won't last forever.

"For our present troubles are quite small and won't last very long. Yet they produce for us an immeasurable great glory that will last forever!"

2 Corinthians 5:17 NLT

During our troubles, we must not diminish our faith. We must realize that there is purpose for the battles. We are to learn from them and be reminded of Jesus's suffering for us. They should give us an opportunity to demonstrate our faith to others and show the power of God working through us.

It is very difficult to face trials, but if we try to understand the lessons involved it is a little easier. The Bible tells us to *"Be joyful whenever you face trials, because testing your faith strengthens you." James 1:2* which can be a difficult scripture to follow, but what it is asking us to do is to be aware of all of the other blessings in our life throughout our struggle. We must trust God and have an unwavering commitment to lean on Him. We should be encouraged daily that no matter what we are facing, God knows our situation. God is willing and able to provide for us, protect us, and bring all we face to a triumphant end. All we have to do is take refuge in Him and trust Him. We may not know exactly how God is going to solve our problems, but we must just stay strong in faith and know that He will do it, in His way and in His timing.

> *"Blessed is the man who remains steadfast under trial, for when he has stood the test he will receive the crown of life, which God has promised to those who love Him."*

James 1:12 ESV

Ask Yourself:

1) When God spoke, Joshua listened and obeyed. Can you think of a time when you felt God speaking to you? Were you obedient to what you heard?
2) It is easy, during trials, to blame God or be angry with Him and turn away. That is just what the enemy wants us to do! He wants us to abandon our faith and not trust God. Scripture tells us

that nothing can separate us from God. He is always with us. What devices of the adversary (or our own human understanding) cause us to lose faith and not trust God?

3) Have you ever experienced a battle that kept coming back? Why do you think it kept happening? How would you approach the battle differently if it came up again?

4) Fortunately, our battles won't last forever. "For our present troubles are quite small and won't last very long. Yet they produce for us an immeasurable great glory that will last forever!" (2 Corinthians 5:17) When you read this scripture, what does it say to you?

5) What are our weapons of warfare as we battle the trials in our lives?

Pray: Father God, the battle belongs to You, but encourage us to pray and to have courage.

Draw near to us in our weakness and strengthen us by the power of Your Holy Spirit. Use the trials in our lives to strengthen our faith and to develop a deep trust in You. We know from Your word that Your ways are perfect, all Your promises come true, and You are a shelter of comfort for those who seek You. You will never forsake or abandon us, no, in fact You have promised to be with us always. We bless and praise Your Holy name, Jesus Christ the Messiah! Thank you, the Lord of Heaven's army for fighting our battles. Amen

"Bridesmaids"

*"Then the Kingdom of Heaven will be like ten bridesmaids
who took their lamps and went to meet the bridegroom."*

Matthew 25:1 NLT

THE BRIDE IS hidden away from the guests as the church fills with the invitees to the sacred event. Not everyone is invited. An exquisite invitation arrived at the invitee's house a time and time ago, with their name called out on a linen envelope. The called ones were presented with a choice as to whether or not they would attend the wedding event. Those who have responded yes to the invitation have now gathered at this specific date and time, with delight and anticipation; eager for the music to announce the bride's arrival.

Her bridesmaids smile, and delight in the bride's beauty. She is beautifully adorned, and has never looked so lovely. The groom and his attendants stand ready to proceed with the ceremony. The bride peeks from around the corner of the foyer, hoping to catch a glimpse of the festivities, but the bridesmaids hold her back. The bridesmaids await their cue from the master of ceremonies as to when to begin the procession down the aisle toward the altar. The bridesmaids must enter first.

The bridesmaids always precede the bride.

Who are the bridesmaids? They are the beloved friends of the bride. Some are new friends, and some are old friends, or relatives she has had for a lifetime. They may or may not know each other, but they all share a love for the bride. It is a unique time, when the bridesmaids will sacrificially lay down their own beauty, individuality, and agendas to magnify the bride. They will don the same dress, the same jewelry, the same hairdo, and because of the loving request of the bride, they will obediently wear the clothing, make-up, or hairdo that might even be unflattering, in order to demonstrate their love for her. They are willing to become less, in order for the bride's beauty and her preferences to dominate the vision for the wedding. It is her special day. Even if a friend is acting like a "Bridezilla," friends will generally concede to the bride's vision for the sacred event.

Scripture talks about bridesmaids too.

> *"Then the Kingdom of Heaven will be like ten bridesmaids*
> *who took their lamps and went to meet the bridegroom."*

> *Matthew 25:1 NLT*

Some Bibles have translated the passage above as ten virgins, instead of bridesmaids. Taking that into context, I have always interpreted the ten virgins as the ones waiting to be the betrothed to the bridegroom; that the five wise bridesmaids represented the remnant of the church who waited eagerly for the return of their Beloved, and so they were prepared for Christ's return.

Yet I have had the epiphany that while, yes, it is a message to the church, more importantly it is a parable explaining the role of pastors, ministry, and church leaders. I would love to present my theory, based on the history and role of bridesmaids when accompanied by scripture.

Firstly, we must establish that the "Bride of Christ," the church, is the entire body of believers.

> *Let us be glad and rejoice, and let us honor Him. For the time*
> *has come for the wedding feast of the Lamb, and His bride has*

prepared herself. She has been given the finest pure white linen to wear. For the fine linen represents the goods deeds of God's holy people."

Revelation 19:7-8 NLT

"Husbands, love your wives, just as Christ loved the church and gave Himself up for her to make her holy, cleansing her by the washing with water through the word, and to present her to Himself as a radiant church, without stain or wrinkle or any other blemish, but holy and blameless."

Ephesians 5:25-27 NIV

*"Come, I will show you the bride, the wife of the Lamb."
And he carried me away in the Spirit to a mountain great and high, and showed me the Holy City, Jerusalem, coming down out of Heaven from God ...Nothing impure will ever enter it, nor will anyone who does what is shameful or deceitful, but only those whose names are written in the Lamb's book of life."*

Revelations 21: 9-27 NIV

Jesus's marriage covenant is with all believers, and is ceremonially represented through communion and taking of the sacraments. The drinking of wine from the cup in remembrance of Christ and His sacrifice, also imitates the ancient Jewish custom of initiating the engagement contract between a bride and groom. According to custom, the couple would recite a betrothal benediction over the glass of wine, and then drink, sealing the contract. In fact, the engaged couple would not drink wine together again until the wedding ceremony, where a cup of wine is shared between bride and groom during the conclusion of the sacred event.

Symbolically, our taking of communion enacts the promise and re-membrance of our own betrothal to the Lamb of God. See Jesus's words to us from the last Passover meal He shared with the apostles.

> *"I tell you, I will not drink from this fruit of the*
> *vine from now on until that day when I drink it*
> *new with you in my Father's Kingdom."*

Matthew 26:29 NIV

Now let us look at a few more verses from Matthew 25.

> *"Then the Kingdom of Heaven will be like ten bridesmaids*
> *who took their lamps and went to meet the bridegroom.*
> *Five of them were foolish, and five were wise. The five*
> *who were foolish didn't take enough olive oil for their*
> *lamps, but the other five were wise enough to take along*
> *extra oil. When the bridegroom was delayed, they*
> *all became drowsy and fell asleep."*

Matthew 25:1-5 NLT

Oil can symbolically represent the anointing, the supernatural pres-ence, of God in one's life. Historically, oil was used for cooking, light-ing lamps, and the sanctification of priests and leaders by the Jewish people. The Parable of the Wise and Foolish Bridesmaids goes on to describe that five of the bridesmaids were prepared for the return of the groom.

Five is the number symbolic of grace in scripture, while ten rep-resents both the law and community. It takes a minyan, ten people by Jewish tradition, to come into communal agreement, in order to ap-proach God in matters of Torah. In this parable we see that by grace, five bridesmaids were able to approach the bridegroom: five in agreement, five dressed, five with oil in their lamps, five with extra oil, were able to approach the bridegroom in this parable. But where was the bride? Why is the bride not mentioned? Where did the extra oil come from?

Psalm 133 speaks about supernatural oil which comes from heaven, perhaps from God's own heart? It is oil birthed from the unity of His children. It is oil that is poured on the heads of God's priests that is in such abundance; yes, so much extra oil that it soaks the garments of the leader.

> *"How good and pleasant it is when God's people live together in unity! It is like precious oil poured on the head, running down on the beard, running down on Aaron's beard, down on the collar of his robe"*

> *Psalm 133:1-2 NIV*

Perhaps it is a time for our leaders to take heed to the customary practices of bridesmaid traditions? Is it time for our leaders to set aside their differences for the honor of the bride, the sheep, and their followers, so the world will know "Christians" by our love?

Is it time to get ready to walk down the aisle in unity? Is it a time to gather in prayer and unity in seeking the supernatural oil of God's blessing, so the bridesmaids are ready for the groom's return? Will individual church communities and leaders be willing to put on the garments of love and walk side-by-side with those who love the bride too?

Is it possible if only five of the ten, or 50%, of the leaders, would gather in unity, that the bridegroom would draw nearer like the parable suggests? The groom is waiting for the procession. Heaven's instruments are being tuned to release the most beautiful music to accompany the bridesmaids. The Master of ceremonies is watching the bridesmaids to see if they will signal Him that the bride is prepared. Heightened anticipation fills the air.

The hit movie "Bridesmaids" showed the wacky pettiness and jealousy that can arise between fellow bridesmaids. The movie amusingly portrayed all the insecurities of the women chosen to stand with the bride on the most important day of her life. We laughed, judged, cringed, and related to some of the emotions portrayed by the characters in the movie, but most importantly we celebrated the triumph of their love over their differences when the five bridesmaids pulled it together to help a weary and nervous bride get through the marriage ceremony. There would have been no wedding unless the bridesmaids assisted the bride.

Unity was the key.

I believe that church leaders who represent the five wise bridesmaids with oil in their lamps are the ones who are willing to work and walk together in unity for the love of the bride. Leaders need to understand the greater authority and call they have to regions, and not just their specific churches or ministries. Jesus said, *"The Kingdom of Heaven is like…" so* we are to be *"Kingdom"* minded. Church communities need to support the local pastoral leadership for establishing a "Christ-centered like-mindedness vision" for a region.

Unity, like the preparation of oil, cannot be done hastily. There must be a time of "pressing" into the heart of God through prayer, praise, and worship. Relationship and trust must be achieved. Neither of these is acquired overnight; that is why the five prepared bridesmaids could not share their oil with the foolish others at the last minute. One's intimacy with God or one another is not something you can give away; both are nurtured through an active, personal relationship.

So, blow the trumpet! Awaken the bridesmaids! Get dressed and fill your lamps with the oil of unity, because the Kingdom of Heaven is near. Bridesmaids, clothe yourselves with love and grace. Put on the fragrance of agreement and prepare the procession. Church: pray for your leaders! All of Heaven waits in the pews as witnesses, ready for the ceremony to begin. Remember, the bridesmaids always precede the bride.

"My prayer is not for them alone. I pray also for those who will believe in Me through their message, that all of them may be one, Father, just as You are in Me and I am in You. May they also be in Us so that the world may believe that You have sent Me. I have given them the glory that You gave Me, that they may be one as We are One—I in them and You in Me—so that they may be brought to complete unity. Then the world will know that You sent Me and have loved them even as You have loved Me."

John 17:20-23 NIV

Ask Yourself:

1) Are you ready for the return of Jesus, the Heavenly Bridegroom? What evidence is there in your life that you are prepared for His coming?

2) Also, what are you doing to be prepared for His coming? How are you helping and encouraging others to be ready? What petty squabbling amongst the other bridesmaids....the other believers in Jesus...can you reduce or even eliminate?

3) What does it mean to say, "They'll know we are Christians by our love?" What changes does that demand of the ways we speak, think, and act? What part of your life will you commit to change today to be ready for the Bridegroom to appear?

4) How could you support and encourage local pastors outside of your own church family to come together in worship and fellowship?

Pray: Heavenly Father, I ask You to make me an instrument of love, peace and unity. My the lamp of my life be filled to the brim with the holy, soothing oil of Your spirit and grace, and may I shed the light of it all around me, especially in the life of Your Bride, the Church. Come, Lord Jesus. Come. Heavenly Bridegroom, come! We long to see Your face! Make us ever more prepared, every day. In Jesus' holy and Matchless name....Amen!

"Cheer"

"When doubts filled my mind, Your comfort gave me renewed
hope and cheer".

Psalm 94:19 NLT

WHO ARE YOU rooting for? Everyone has a home team and everyone loves to cheer them on! We raise our voices and loudly shout words of encouragement towards our champions of the sporting world. Arenas are filled with fans who brandish proof of their enthusiasm toward the action on the playing fields. Huge foam "hands" hold the pointer finger in the up position. "We're Number One!" is yelled by the crowds. Colorful pom-pom-wielding cheerleaders and clever mascots ramp up our praise and admiration of our favorite team. Sports fans are not the only ones who cheer people on. Parents constantly root for the success and well-being of their children. Business owners cheer on their employees. Wives cheer for their husband's success and well-being, and friends support one another for a multitude of common goals and aspirations. Pastors work towards inspiring their congregations, and church members rally for their leadership teams and shared purposes.

Do you know that there is a cloud of witnesses and a God who is rooting for you? Do you understand there is posse of prayer warriors who storm the heavens on others' behalf on a daily basis? Do you hear the rallying cry of the fans and the Lord cheering you on?

"Therefore, since we are surrounded by such a great cloud of witnesses, let us throw off everything that hinders and the sin that so easily entangles, and let us run with perseverance the race marked out for us."

Hebrews 12:1 NIV

"See the flags waving as the enemy attacks. Cheer them on, O Israel! Wave to them as they march against Babylon to destroy the palaces of the high and mighty."

Isaiah 13:2 NLT

"On that day the announcement to Jerusalem will be, "Cheer up, Zion! Don't be afraid!"

Zephaniah 3:16 NLT

The Lord is specific in personally cheering for you and me. In fact He will even put enthusiastic "cheerleaders" into our lives to encourage us and be our traveling companions on the playing field of life. We all have feelings of being overwhelmed, exhausted, financially pressured, and stressed that interfere with our game playing, but we must remain focused and listen to the voice of the crowd cheering us to victory. We must learn to heed the encouragement of the fans, and discern the voice of the opponent.

Yes, there exist devices and lies of the adversary which will provoke even the staunchest believer to be taken out of the game and benched on the sidelines. By our own wrong assumptions we can mistakenly enter into a relationship with God and the church with unreasonable expectations. We do not count the cost of following Christ with devoted obedience. Players can let us down with bad sportsmanship, or the disappointment of failure, betrayal, and offense amongst the team members. Deferred hope or lack of provision for the completion of a dream can crush motivation for both the cheerleader and team player. Our love and loyalty as a fan can wane through the course of our lives due to our own personal experiences. Sometimes legacy, allegiance, tradition, culture, and community are still not enough to keep us interested in the action on the field. One can become weary in the journey and feel isolated and alone. In order to be conquerors we must fix our vision on the goal and not the battle, and of course, we must remember who is playing on our team and who is in the grandstands cheering for us.

> *"Then Elisha prayed, "O LORD, open his eyes and let him see!"*
> *The LORD opened the young man's eyes, and when he looked*
> *up, he saw that the hillside around Elisha was filled with*
> *horses and chariots of fire."*

> *2 Kings 6:17 NLT*

> *"What shall we say about such wonderful things as these?*
> *If God is for us, who can ever be against us?*

> *Romans 8:31 NLT*

Life is a journey. There are no guarantees, except that we do not have to do it alone. God is with us always and He hears our prayer. Look what encouragers had to say in the scriptures below.

> *"Eli said, "Cheer up! May the God of Israel grant the request*
> *you have asked of Him."*

> *1 Samuel 1:17 NLT*

"When Jesus heard him, He stopped and said, "Tell him to come here." So they called the blind man. "Cheer up," they said. "Come on, He's calling you!"

Mark 10:49 NLT

It's minutes before the final whistle is blown, and the concentration of the team players is intensely focused on the goal at hand. They know they will only be victorious if they can move as a team. Unity is paramount. Silent signs, plans, and strategies are exchanged between the head coach and the team captains. The team captains call the plays and release the other players into play on the field. The fans in the stands raise their voices in one accord shouting, "Victory! Victory!" Unbelief is set aside; faith arises as the crowd rallies to witness the approaching battle. Unity, one mind, one heart, and one goal is preeminent. Will the players remember that all things are possible? Will they remember their training? Will the odds be overcome?

Transparently I lay before you the team that I am rooting for. I guess you would call them the "Saints". Their head coaches are the Father, Son, and Holy Spirit. Their game strategies are shared in the Word and during prayer time. The team captains are our loving community of pastors, and every believer is a potential teammate on the field. Believers are also the fans (accompanied by the witnesses in Heaven and the Holy Host of angels) cheering from the stands. I want to encourage each of us to put on our colors, equip ourselves with the word of God, pick up a pom-pom and get into the game. May we love our *team* (God) with all our heart, all our mind, all our spirit, and all our strength; and may we love one another. May our team spirit unite us to take new and higher ground for the Lord's glory! May the Lord ignite a fire in our bellies to not be satisfied with the status quo, but instead to go for the ultimate conquest...the hearts of *all* men and women in our communities. They will know us by our love and by our ability to unite as one under the headship of Jesus Christ. Jesus is cheering for you, me, and all of us! Don't doubt His love or plans for your life.

So, "Go, Team!" Cheer along with me, "We got the fire (Holy FIRE), we're hot, we can't be stopped!" and "You can do it, you can do it! You can, you can!" Yes, let us shout and cheer each other along for His Kingdom's purposes and His glory, and may our cities be devoted to the Lord.

Go Saints!

> *"On the seventh day, they got up at daybreak and marched around the city seven times in the same manner, except that on that day they circled the city seven times. The seventh time around, when the priests sounded the trumpet blast, Joshua commanded the army, "Shout! For the Lord has given you the city! The city and all that is in it are to be devoted to the Lord."*
>
> *Joshua 6:15-17 NIV*

Ask Yourself:

1) Who are the cheerleaders in your life? Who provides encouragement for your struggles? Have you thanked them?
2) For whom are you a source of encouragement? Have you let them know you're cheering for them?
3) Who can you call today to offer a word of encouragement and support? Do it now!

Pray: Lord, I am grateful for every supporter and cheerleader You have led into my life. Let me be that sort of aid and encouragement to others! Show me right now who needs to hear a word of cheer from me. Help me to mean it....and work towards it...when I pray, 'Your Kingdom come.... Your will be done....on earth, as it is in Heaven!' Amen.

"Covenant"

"Then He took the cup, and when He had given thanks, He gave it to them, saying, "Drink from it, all of you. This is My blood of the covenant, which is poured out for many for the forgiveness of sins."

Matthew 26:27-28 NIV

WITH THE START of the New Year, we often find ourselves creating our own covenants, promises or New Year's resolutions. We set promises to lose weight and get into shape, to spend less and give more, to read a book or study His word daily, or to clean house, to strive to be more obedient to the Ten Commandments, to love more deeply, and forgive more generously. Still, something often interferes with our plan or promise, and we quit. So what is a covenant, and what do we need to do to stick with it and not quit?

A covenant is a legally binding obligation, a promise, and an act of faith, trust and obedience. Have you ever made a promise and backed out of it? Has someone ever promised you something and let you down? Has someone broken covenant with you? Did you break a covenant oath with another? Keeping our promises can be very challenging if we rely only on our emotions and will power. I do believe that most people have the best intentions; but unfortunately things like carnal temptations, human reasoning, deception, earthly understandings, and free will can take our hearts and minds away from our promises. We can fail. Like all relationships, there must be a coming together of our personalities to operate in harmony. In a perfect world we would be of like mind and faith, and promises would always succeed. Unfortunately we don't live in a perfect world and people grow weary. They lack steadfast faith, and they throw in the towel.

When Moses fled Egypt to Mount Sinai with the Israelites, God made a covenant with His people.

> *"Now if you obey Me and keep My covenant, you will be My own special treasure from among all the nations of the earth; for all the earth belongs to Me and you will be to Me a Kingdom of priests, My holy nation. Give this message to the Israelites."*

> *Exodus 19:5-6 NLT*

> *"Moses shared this new covenant with the Israelites and their response was favorable. We will do everything the Lord has commanded."*

> *Exodus 19:8 NLT*

During this time the Israelites were given the Ten Commandments and serious instructions on how to live a holy and pure life. They were being groomed to meet God.

Are you groomed to meet God? What condition is your faith in and are you holding up your end of the covenants that God has made with you, and that you have made with others?

After two years in the desert, the Israelites began to grow weary. They complained. They were disobedient. They actually thought living as slaves in Egypt was better than the life they were living at that point. Their lack of faith and trust in God caused fear and hard hearts, so consequently they were not permitted to enter the Promised Land; the

Land of Milk and Honey. God was upset His People had broken their covenant, and consequently their actions led to forty years of wandering in the wilderness.

> *"Now tell them this: "As surely as I live, declares the Lord,*
> *I will do to you the very things I heard you say. You will all*
> *drop dead in this wilderness! Because you complained against*
> *Me, every one of you who is twenty years old or older and was*
> *included in the registration will die. You will not enter and*
> *occupy the land I swore to give you. The only exceptions will be*
> *Caleb son of Jephunneh and Joshua son of Nun."*

Numbers 14:28-30 NLT

Have you ever grown weary of a situation; been so disappointed by yourself or someone else that you quit? Well, the Israelites quit. Their fear and lack of trust in God kept them in the wilderness. And they let God down. Because of their hard hearts and unwillingness to trust Him, they suffered for forty years. What happened to their faith? What happened to their commitment to "Do everything that the Lord asked of them?" Their eyes were not focused on doing God's will, and their minds were clouded with selfish reasoning that got them nowhere. They failed to live up to God's covenant. Didn't the Israelites want to be "God's Special Treasures," and to live in the "Land of Milk and Honey?" The breaking of covenant changed their God ordained destiny. The fear and covenant breaking forfeited God's ability to bless the naysayers.

So, how do we hold on to our faith and not end up like the Israelites, wandering the desert for forty years, missing our destiny? Let's look at the two Israelites who earned God's favor. Caleb and Joshua were faithful servants. Caleb and Joshua were two of the twelve men sent to scout the Land of Canaan, the Promised Land. They represented the two tribes of Judah and Ephraim.

"The Lord said to Moses send the men to explore the Land of Canaan, the land I am giving to Israel. Send one leader from each tribe of the twelve ancestral tribes."

Numbers 13:2 NLT

After returning from Canaan, the men reported back to Moses.

"... We arrived in the land you sent us to see, and it is indeed a magnificent country- a land flowing with milk and honey. Here is some of the fruit we have brought as proof. But the people living there are powerful and their cities and towns are fortified and very large."

Numbers 13:27-28 TLB

The majority of Israelite leaders were concerned and afraid.

"... We can't go up against them! The land we explored will swallow up any who go to live there. All the people we saw are huge. We even saw giants...We felt like grasshoppers next to them and that's what we look like to them."

Numbers 13:31-33 NLT

Caleb tried hard to encourage them.

".... Let's go at once to take the land,' he said. 'We can certainly conquer it!'"

Numbers 13:30 NLT

Caleb and Joshua chose to honor a great God. I bet Caleb and Joshua's faith wasn't any greater than the other Israelites; but rather, they were men of faith who wanted to glorify a Great God and had no choice but to serve Him with complete obedience. Both Caleb and Joshua trusted God, as they knew in their hearts that God was completely trustworthy. Therefore, they could act with assurance and boldness and not be afraid.

In addition to drawing strength from Caleb and Joshua, we can also learn from the parable of the Mustard Seed. The Mustard Seed is the smallest of all seeds. And Jesus uses this seed to show just what can grow from even the smallest of life.

> *"The Kingdom of Heaven is like a Mustard Seed planted in a field. It is the smallest of all seeds but it becomes the largest of garden plant and grows into a tree where birds can come and find shelter in its branches."*
>
> *Matthew 13:31 NLT*

This covenant that God created for the Israelites should remind us there is great hope and promise in our future if we focus our eyes on God's will and be obedient to His ways and not our own. We must not be led by emotions which can hinder our ability to keep the faith, and hold the course. Therefore trust in Him as we enter into each New Year and we approach our New Year's Resolutions or promises - be it with ourselves, our families, our spouse, or with God - let us find the faith that Caleb and Joshua had, let our hearts move mountains by growing steadfast in love...growth akin to a small mustard seed... and let our obedience to God lead us to the Land of Milk and Honey. May our covenant promises be treasured and lead to living in fulfilled destiny.

"The joy of the Lord be your strength."

Nehemiah 8:10 NLT

Ask Yourself:

1) The Israelites struggled with doubting the promises of God that He would take them to a new land, where they would be free and prosper. What things in your life contribute to you doubting the promises of God that He wants for you?

2) What tools can help us move forward in our faith in God and His promises and also in other commitments, covenants and personal relationships?

3) Do you relate more to the faith of the Israelites or to the faith shown by Caleb and Joshua? Why?

4) What is a resolution that you can apply to yourself that will help you grow closer to God?
Are there broken covenants that you need to reflect, repent, forgive, and bring before the Lord for complete healing?

Pray: Lord, I know You are always faithful in keeping Your promises. I desire to be faithful and trustworthy too. Help me with this resolution to trust You at all times, and by making that faith the most important part of every day, enable me to be a strong witness to Your loving covenant to all who meet me. Please forgive any of my broken covenants with You or others. In Jesus' Loving name...Amen!

"Done"

"As for God, His way is upright" the word of God is pure;
He is a shield to all those who take refuge in Him."

Psalm 18:30 NIV

"DONE!" WAS THE reply of the waitress when my husband asked for a cup of coffee.

"What?" he asked incredulously.

She replied again, "Coffee, done!" and she turned her back and walked away from the table in the restaurant where he was seated. It was finished. There was nothing more to be said, but that did not sit well with my husband.

"How could that be?" was his next thought, and more importantly, "Where am I going to get a cup of coffee on this remote island in the Caribbean?"

Many times as a believer I am confronted with this same attitude in myself and others. The waitress responded from her experience, reality, or scientific facts that the coffee was done. No more. And my husband was out of luck. Yet, as a believer we know that we have something better than luck. We can walk by faith and see clearly what the Lord has revealed to us. We do not have to struggle with human understanding, but instead we can reach beyond our earthly vision and see the plans God has for us. I encourage each of us to dig deeper into the well of

Jesus when we become so thirsty that it is unbearable. There have been many times where I have been "done" with my own devices, and then led lovingly to surrender to God in order for Him to move on my behalf. I needed to understand that I had run out of solutions, tactics, schemes, plans, and provisions for changing the circumstances with which I struggled, and that I needed His intervention. My heartfelt cry became, *"Lord my resources are gone, my pockets are empty, in fact there seems to be holes in them. I am heartbroken, exhausted, and I am so done! Please hear my prayer and move on my behalf. You are my only resource. You are my only hope. May Your Kingdom come, may Your will be done!"*

If you struggle with unbelief, or encounter unbelief in others, don't be discouraged! Go back to the source of "Living Water." He will quench your thirst. Pray again. *"If it be Your will, increase my faith, Lord. Remove the unbelief, and help me to fix my eyes on You. You, Lord, is where my help will come from, and through Your Holy Spirit my cup will run over! May Your will be done!"*

> *"The Lord is my shepherd, I lack nothing. He makes me lie down in green pastures, He leads me beside quiet waters, He refreshes my soul. He guides me along the right paths for His name's sake. Even though I walk through the darkest valley, I will fear no evil, for You are with me; Your rod and Your staff, they comfort me. You prepare a table before me in the presence of my enemies. You anoint my head with oil; my cup runneth over. Surely Your goodness and love will follow me all the days of my life, and I will dwell in the house of the Lord forever."*

Psalm 23 NIV

Ask Yourself:

1) What dead ends, what road blocks have you faced in your life?
2) How did those situations get resolved? Did you see the hand of the Lord in the outcome? Or are you still confused about them?
3) What are you dealing with today that seems beyond your ability or even your comprehension? What do you hear the voice of God saying to you about it? Trust me? Have patience? I have a better plan?

Pray: Lord, You already know the problems and issues in my life that are way outside my resources. Can You help me to trust You more today? Restore in me the joy of my salvation, so that nothing....nothing...disturbs my peace and contentment. I love You, Lord, and I want to be wholly Yours, no matter what I feel because of my worries and doubts. Show me right now Your loving touch in my life so that my faith is strengthened and my hope renewed. In the Matchless name of Jesus....Amen!

"Father"

---

*"I will be a Father to you, and you will be My sons and
daughters, says the Lord Almighty."*

2 Corinthians 6:18 NIV

EVERYONE HAS A biological father. Even the person who has been conceived artificially carries the DNA of a male. No one would exist without the contribution from a man to a woman's pregnancy. That is except Adam, Eve, and of course, Jesus, who was conceived in Mary by the power of the Holy Spirit. Jesus' spirit carried the DNA of the divine, but His flesh was wholly human and genetically descended from Abraham, King David, and the tribe of Judah. Adam came from the dust of the Earth, and Eve from out of Adam's rib, and the Lord breathed life into both of their bodies.

My point is this: we all have beginnings that are out of our control. We don't get to choose our fathers, or how we are conceived, but even so, God is sovereign over all. He has a plan for each one of us. He has a purpose for us, and He wants a relationship with us. He wants us to know Him as our Heavenly Father.

The father-child relationship is huge, and probably impacts our lives greater than any other relationship that we have. Ideally a child is conceived in love and raised in a family environment that fosters trust, learning, and the positive development to become a rational functioning person in society. Unfortunately, this scenario is true in only some instances. Life is complicated and children are born into such varying situations that having the ideal is just a fairy tale. Children grow up with no father, step fathers, or adoptive fathers, or maybe just a spiritual father from church, or a family friend as a father role-model. Some children may feel that they have never felt the love or care from their father figures. Even so, all fathers will naturally fail at meeting *all* the needs of their children. They may struggle with providing for the family financially or because of their own brokenness or cultural upbringing fail to emotionally connect with their children. Fathers are human, and vulnerable to making mistakes. Fathers are not perfect, even if some think they are. I think all of us can reflect on times when we have either felt rejected, angry, disappointed, frustrated, hopeless, abandoned, unprotected, or hurt by our relationship with our fathers. Yet the Bible says we should honor them.

"Honor your father…"

Exodus 20:12 NIV

"Honor your father and mother. Love your neighbor as yourself.' "

Matthew 19:19 NLT

We need to also acknowledge that many fathers strive to serve their families with all their strength and have made incredible investments into their children's lives. We honor them with thankful hearts, while we try to forgive our fathers where they have not fulfilled their God intended role. The wonderful news is that we have a perfect Father in Heaven that is easy to honor!!

"I will be a Father to you, and you will be My sons and daughters, says the Lord Almighty."

2 Corinthians 6:18 NIV

"How great is the love the Father has lavished on us,
that we should be called children of God! And that
is what we are! The reason the world does not know
us is that it did not know Him."

1 John 3:1 NIV

"For you did not receive a spirit that makes you a slave again
to fear, but you received the Spirit of sonship. And by Him we
cry, "Abba," Father."

Romans 8:15 RSVCE

Through Jesus Christ's sacrifice on the cross at Calvary, we have been adopted by the King of Heaven, the Author of Life, and the Creator of the Universe. He is the "dream" Father, and He is not a fairy tale, but *real*. By receiving Christ into our hearts we establish and reconcile our relationship with God the Father. We miraculously become His children. We become His sons and daughters. Outside of Christ we are just God's prodigals and not yet legal heirs to our inheritance.

Our inheritance is a life forgiven of sin, salvation, and eternity in Heaven in the presence of God.

In fact, one will ultimately receive eternal judgment instead of mercy apart from a relationship with Jesus Christ. Although the Lord's grace and patience allows Him to shower blessings on both the good and evil in this world, it will only be with a repentant heart that anyone can truly become an official child of God. Having a relationship with your heavenly Father is as simple as bowing your head, asking for forgiveness, and accepting Jesus as your Savior. Believing in Christ begins the best loving Father-child relationship that you could ever imagine. I encourage you to do so. Let Him into your heart and let Him love on you, as only a Father can do. May you feel His loving arms around you as He whispers His awesome plans for your life!

"May our Lord Jesus Christ Himself and God our Father, Who loved us and by His grace gave us eternal encouragement and good hope."

2 Thessalonians 2:16 NIV

"My Father, who has given them to Me, is greater than all; no one can snatch them out of My Father's hand."

John 10:29 NIV

Ask Yourself:

1) What words come to mind when you hear the word, 'father?' What are the qualities of an ideal father? Loving, caring, compassionate, generous, patient....? What is your strongest memory of the most significant father-figure in your life?

2) What words come to mind when you hear the title, 'Heavenly Father?' Jesus showed us how to have a relationship with our Heavenly Father. What aspects of His character do you most need or want to see develop in your own life? Since He's your father, the more you are around Him the more you will come to imitate Him.

3) Do you see differences and/or similarities between an earthly 'father' and 'Heavenly Father?'

4) What scriptures assure you of a loving relationship with your Heavenly Father?

5) If you don't believe you have a relationship with your Heavenly Father, how can you begin one....right now? Invite Jesus into your heart!!!

6) Around you are friends and acquaintances who have a father-wound. They may be afraid of God as a Father because their own experience with an earthly father whom was not a blessing. What

about God's love and concern can you show them as you share the Father in Heaven with them today?

Pray: Heavenly Father, I love it that You love me as Your own dear child. I love it that You will always be patient and kind and caring with me, no matter how many times I fall or fail. Let me so accept and trust in You as the perfect Father that You shine out of my life into a hurting world. Make me so aware of Your love today that people will ask why I'm so happy. In the name of Your only-begotten Son, my Savior, Jesus...Amen!

"Favorite"

---~---

"… you both have the same Master in Heaven, and He has no favorites."

Ephesians 6:9 NLT

CHRISTMAS MORNING WE wake up expectant and rush into the traditional activities of celebration, worship, gift giving, family, and a special meal prepared for the day. Inevitably, at the end of the day, everyone reflects on their favorite gifts given and received, their favorite tasty morsels devoured, their favorite funny family moments, their favorite Christmas movies, favorite Christmas songs, favorite Christmas message, and the list goes on. I want to believe that we want to remember and catalog the best, the sacred, and the goodness of the celebration of Christ's birthday. Most people want to fall asleep on the evening of the 25th "with visions of sugar plums dancing in their heads," but that is not how it always goes down. Even with a worshipful and grateful heart, human brokenness and unmet expectations can whisper into our hearts and mind, and become a stronghold.

People and relationships are messy. We seem to be a complete bundle of emotional ganglia and sensitivity during the holidays. Childhood relationships tend to grow into adult liabilities, and if relational conflict issues are not resolved properly, insecurities can abound. It can be very easy to slip into self-pity, anger, and disappointment if holiday gatherings focus too intently on gift exchanges, past histories, or un-constructive verbal discord. Let's face the fact that most of us have a family member that can suck all the oxygen out of the room by just entering it.

How does one cope with rejection and un-forgiveness from a loved one at a family gathering? How do you forgive hurt caused to you in the past, and then set yourself up for further injury by encountering the offender at an upcoming gathering? How do you stand by and watch parental favoritism pass you by, while it is distributed through the love language of gifts unto others? How does one cope with the jealousy and self-condemnation it inspires?

Christians joyfully celebrate the good fortune of others, but it is a struggle when you or your children have personally been cheated or over-looked by a loved one. How does one not want to throw "the Favorite" into the pit, which was the fate of Joseph from the Bible? How do you get rid of the feelings of unworthiness and frustration and mis-directed anger at the "Favorite?" Can we not allow the relative to have a favorite? And if you are a favorite, how can you be sensitive to others around you and not further provoke hurt feelings? As we know, everyone has favorites. Maybe not favorite parents, children, or grandchildren, but being undeniably drawn to someone and or something in particular is a human quality. Life is just not fair most times, nor is everyone treated equally.

Praise God, our God is not human.

Our God loves each of us unconditionally and sees us through the lens of His Son. He sees us perfected through the obedient, loving, and sacrificial life of Jesus. God loves us without favoritism. Although scripture will show that *God's favor* can be selective on individual's lives, His love is without favorites. He is impartial and would give His own life, the most treasured gift of all, for each of us. Salvation and everlasting life is our Lord's favorite gift to give. He came on Christmas Day so *all* could be saved.

"God so loved the world that He gave His one and only begotten Son, so that whoever believes in Him should not perish but have everlasting life."

John 3:16 NKJV

Human emotions can get the best of us. I challenge each of us, who profess Christ, to try to emulate Jesus, and to take our hurt to the foot of the cross. We have to learn to die to our emotional reactions for the sake of harmony and love of others. Be slow to anger. Choose to focus on Christ and His love for you, rather than disappointment or hurt. Strive to be impossible to offend, and quick to forgive the offender. Remember, they are only human, as are you. Exchange the bitterness for allowing Jesus to fill your heart with so much revelation of His love for you that the disappointments of this world become chaff; that the offenses become as fragile as dandelions that can be blown away with one big breath of understanding and love. The favor of the Lord comes through our obedience to walk in His ways…and He calls us to love…even those who are our enemies. This can only be accomplished through faith, prayer, and focusing on Christ. My prayer is that all of us can enter into each Christmas season with a refreshed knowledge of peace and an understanding of God's steadfast love that comes from walking through life holding His hand. That we see ourselves through His eyes and through the revelation of His Holy word.

Ask Yourself:

1) In your family were you the more favored or less favored?
2) How do you want God to show that He believes you are special and valued by Him?
3) How can you show God's love and care to someone else today?
4) How can you let go of any jealousy you may have toward a "favorite" in your own family?

Pray: Abba Father, We trust You and know that You love us unconditionally, we receive Your love and favor, as You deem to release it to us: through Your gracious hands…in Your perfect timing. Forgive us for our anger and frustrations at others, and remove the hurt from our hearts that we may walk with clean hands and pure hearts before You. Thank you Lord, that You don't have favorites, but love each of us unconditionally, giving us the greatest gift of all: Your love. In Jesus' name...Amen.

"...Teacher, we know how honest You are. You teach about the way of God regardless of the consequences. You are impartial and don't play favorites."

Matthew 22:16 NLT

"And remember that the heavenly Father to whom you pray has no favorites. He will judge... "

1Peter 1:17 NLT

"Honor"

HONOR. HONOR IS an actionable demonstration of our emotions. Honor
is how we feel about someone, and then we demonstrate that honor by
how we interact with that person. By definition honor is to have "high
respect" for someone who has earned it, or has met the qualifications to
be respected by others. We can see "honor" demonstrated in our court-
rooms when we refer to the judges as "His Honorable judge *So and So.*"
The judge's position and credentials have earned him the honor of the
people in the court before they even begin proceedings. "Honor" actually precedes the judge's name and lets the courtroom know how to communicate with this person of distinction.

The Hebrew definition of honor comes from the word *Kabad.* It actually describes the weighty authority, respect, responsibility, riches, and
glory which are reserved for honoring God.

Honor and respect are things not modeled too readily in our society
today. Our culture has learned to mock the elderly, to quip back at authority with clever backhanded remarks, to question our employers, teachers,
and police force, to challenge our governing systems, and to criticize our
pastors and rebuke portions of the Bible....just because we feel like it.

Yet God sees things very differently.

"Show proper respect to everyone: Love the family of believers,
fear God, honor the emperor."

1Peter 2:17 NIV

"Love each other with genuine affection and take delight in
honoring each other."

Romans 12:10 NLT

People have a natural way of honoring the individual who has perse-
vered through daunting challenges, or the incredible athlete who has
accomplished great physical feats. We honor poets, writers, scientists,
musicians, actors, philanthropists, inventors, educators, and movie
makers with special ceremonies and pomp and circumstance. But
God asks us to honor everyone, and that includes you. Think about
the people around you that could use a bit of encouragement and respect. Can't we try a little harder to be less critical and more thankful
for the people in our lives? Particularly when looking at ourselves in
the mirror.

How can you honor others if you don't first honor yourself? And how
can you honor yourself…"the created"…if you don't honor "the Creator?"
Is it possible that the Lord is nudging you to spend a little more time in
His presence, His house, His word, so He can reveal Himself to you and
tell you how "fearfully and wonderfully made" you are? How much He
loves you? Everyone is a child of God and worthy of honor, just because
we are His. God shares His honor with us as a free gift. We don't have to
earn it because He did it for us. Jesus honored us by giving everything at
Calvary for us.

"But what we do see is Jesus, Who was made a little lower than
the angels for a little while, now is 'crowned with glory and

honor' because He suffered death, so that by the grace of God
He might taste death for everyone."

Hebrews 2:9 NIV

Remember that honor is bestowed upon someone who has earned the right to be treated that way. Jesus has earned the honor. So, why do we forget so quickly that Jesus is worthy of all our worship, and that He should be a priority of our honor? We are completely unapologetic and culturally numb to letting the little stuff, the "necessary-but mundane-stuff," interfere with our heavenly court dates with the Honorable King of Kings. What if we tried blowing off a court date with one of our local judges? The fact is a local judge probably would not be too full of grace or mercy for the circumstances of our lives that detoured us from showing up in his courtroom. The judge would probably respond with heavy judgment and consequences. So why do we so easily blow off our merciful and gracious God when He calls us into His courtroom? Are we honoring Him by saying, "Later...when it is convenient...when I am ready and feel like it?"

Don't let fear or distractions interfere with you coming into His glorious presence. You can pray and talk to God anytime, and anywhere. We can honor God by responding with grateful respect, and making time in our daily lives to sit in His courtroom. Can you imagine that the Creator of the Universe wants you to spend time with Him? I pray that we will all be moved to honor Him, and to respond to His invitation of intimate relationship. May we too sing with all creation His praises!

"Then I heard every creature in heaven and on earth and
under the earth and on the sea, and all that is in them,
singing: 'To Him who sits on the throne and to the lamb, be all
the praise and honor and glory and power, forever and ever.'"

Revelation 5:13 NIV

Ask Yourself:

1) In your life, who is worthy of honor? Do you make certain they receive it? How?
2) Are there times you have shown God less than the honor He deserves? How?
3) How can you honor God today? Right now?

Pray: Heavenly Father, I honor You for Who You are: Creator and Lord of the Universe. I honor You for what You have done in sending Your Son to die for me. I honor You for giving me the courage, the strength, the wisdom and the faith to get through my struggles. I honor You because You love me unconditionally. Help me, Lord, to model the honor I have for You in my treatment of myself and others. In the holy name of Jesus....Amen!

"Invest"

"Invest in acts of charity. Charity yields high returns."

Ecclesiastes 11:1 MSG

WHAT DO YOU invest in? How do you spend your time, your money, your energy, your thought-life, and your resources? People can invest in many things. We can invest in the pursuit of successful careers, making money, raising children, marriages, education, possessions, and maintenance of homes, the endless pursuit of trying to look attractive and younger, physical exercise, volunteering, cooking, ministry, social activities, and the pursuit of pleasure, entertainment, and recreation. Which of these many things actually retains its "investment value?" Was the dividend long lasting? How much joy and happiness was in the return? The world will tell you if you work hard, and invest your efforts wisely, that you can achieve wealth, success, and happiness. Is this true?

Let's look at the lives of some people who dedicated their lives to investing in some of the pursuits listed above, and see where it took them. A great example is the show Gilligan's Island, where being shipwrecked became the great equalizer for the castaways, just as death will be for all of us. One day we will all stand before God and have to give account how we have spent our lives-what we have invested in. We will have nothing with us from this world except our memories and things of our hearts. Gilligan and the Skipper spent their lives working hard and traveling from port to port. The Professor's passion was science and the pursuit of knowledge. Ginger sought after fame, beauty, and riches, while Mary Anne spent most of her time chasing after the approval of others. The Howells toiled after money, fortune, and luxury; yet on the island each was separated from their prior lives. Their identities, self-worth, and trappings of the world were forced to collide with the truth of the situation. In reality none of them were any different than anyone else on the island. They were all just people. Their "character" was the only lasting thing that was apparent from the lives they used to lead. What would someone say about your character aside from your net worth, beauty aids, clothes and all the activities that keep you busy?

How can we strengthen our character? I believe that the more we strive towards investing in others, with deposits of love, service, mercy, and forgiveness, the more we will fortify our "Christ" nature and glorify God. How do we learn to not be driven by the "American Dream" or the fear of what others may think of us, and just learn seek things of His Kingdom? How do we learn to disconnect our minds from "human reasoning" and learn to connect to "trusting God" in how we invest our time and energy? God promises that all good things come from Him. He is *Jehovah Jireh*; God our provider. He will take care of all our needs, large and small, and that we are never to worry or doubt Him regarding provision and blessing in our lives.

"Seek the Kingdom of God above all else, and He will give you everything you need."

Luke 12:31 NLT

Jesus asked his disciples to walk away from their daily lives. He said, "Come and follow me." He desired them to invest in spending time with Him. They followed Jesus to villages and sites where people's lives were miraculously transformed because of His presence. The disciples learned to trust Jesus to take care of their ordinary daily needs so they could be "present "in the extraordinary life of His ministry. They learned by actively seeking Him first, and desiring His will for their lives. They found their lives transformed. They would never be the same. How sad, and how different their lives would have been if they had allowed their families, careers, commitments, pursuit of money, or fears get in the way of following Jesus.

I pray that all of us have the courage to set aside our personal agendas and pursuits when the voice of the Lord calls to have us invest our time in His Kingdom. May we learn to trust Him and invest in what is best, and in what is sure to reap a plentiful return not only here, but for all eternity.

> *"Command those who are rich in this present world not to be arrogant nor to put their hope in wealth, which is so uncertain, but to put their hope in God, who richly provides us with everything for our enjoyment. Command them to do good, to be rich in good deeds, and to be generous and willing to share. In this way they will lay up treasure for themselves as a firm foundation for the coming age, so that they may take hold of the life that is truly life."*
>
> *1 Timothy 6: 17-19 NIV*

Ask Yourself:

1) What have you 'invested in' in your life?
2) Which of those 'investments' have been worthwhile and valuable, and which not-so-much? What makes the difference?
3) What specific changes to your life is God calling you to 'invest in' today? What things have you invested in that will still be here in one hundred years?

Pray: Lord, I believe Your promises are true. I believe that if I put You first in my life that You will provide peace and joy and contentment. I admit that in the past I have spent, time, money and emotional energy on things that did not satisfy. Remake my focus today, Lord...right now.... so that my heart is directed toward the goals which You value. Help me to fix my eyes on You and the things of Your kingdom. In the name that is above every name: Jesus....Amen!

"Jesus"

"In the beginning the Word already existed. The Word was with God, and the Word was God."

John 1:1 NLT

THERE IS NO other word like "Jesus." Does there exist a more powerful or controversial word? It is a word that is known around the world, and has united and divided nations and cultures. It is a word that can create powerful feelings of hope, misunderstanding, conviction, condemnation, fear, etc.

The Hebrew translation for "the Word" is literally the "agent of creation."

God.

"The Lord merely spoke, and the heavens were created. He breathed the Word, and all the stars were born."

Psalm 33:6 NLT

So why are we surprised when this word, this name, Jesus, creates powerful emotions within us? For those who are at peace with Him, and know Him intimately, this name can mean refuge, rescuer, healer, provider, or comforter. For others, the word Jesus can stir feelings of doubt, unbelief, anger, disdain, or indifference. Two thousand years ago, Jesus asked one of His disciples the question below:

"Then He asked them, "But who do you say I am?" Peter
replied, "You are the Messiah.""

Mark 8:29 NLT

How do you think you might answer that same question? What do you
feel? Peter replied that Jesus was the Messiah. Peter was declaring that
Jesus was the Jewish Savior prophesied by prophets in the holy Torah.
This was a radical and revelatory exclamation two thousand years ago,
and even still today! The Jewish people had been waiting to be rescued
from an oppressive world under the domination of a Roman government. They knew they needed a Savior from Rome, but they did not
know they needed a Savior to bring them back into right relationship
with God.

Do you know that you need a Savior?

"Needing a Savior" is probably an easier concept for women to
grasp than for men. Historically women have always understood that
they can't completely rely on themselves to get through life. Although
women can hold their own intellectually with men, women understand
that men pretty much have them beat in the muscle department, and
that women rely on a man's physical strength in supporting our society.
Sure there are exceptions, but nothing illustrates the strength difference more clearly than when women are pregnant, and become physically vulnerable and limited in the last trimester of their trimester.

Since the beginning, women have searched for a "Savior," a
"Rescuer," to make life easier. Remember it was the women that visited
Jesus' tomb first, and thus saw the resurrected Christ before any of the
men. Their "hope" for the future had just been beaten and hung on
a cross. They deeply mourned the loss of their possible rescuer, and
driven by that emotional need for a Savior, they went to be close to
Him, even if that meant to gather at His burial place. Jesus was the

equalizer. He came and blew the roof off of preconceived notions of "religiousness" and "societal worth." Jesus came and made the "game board of life" a level playing field for men, women, and children, for rich and poor, the young and old, for genetically gifted and the physically and mentally disabled.

He declared that anyone who believes in Him, repents and turns from their wicked ways, can be saved; that He is the Savior of the Jews, yes, but also of the entire world. Jesus is not only available to us now during our lifetimes, but for the future and all eternity. For although Jesus declared Himself Lord two millennia ago...He can be your Lord now if you ask Him into your heart.

Life can feel like one huge intensive chess game, and the strategy and fatigue of playing can wear anyone down in the game of life. The wonderful thing is as a Christian we know our Master is an expert at winning! He is our ace in the hole for overcoming the challenges we face. Yes, Jesus is indeed, the "Lord of Board"...and everyone is invited to play. I hope that you will surrender to the Savior and allow Him to be Lord and Master over your life. Each of us must ask the question, "Who is Jesus to you?"

"Jesus"... There is just something about the Word.

> *"So the Word became human and made His home among us.*
> *He was full of unfailing love and faithfulness. And we have*
> *seen His glory, the glory of the Father's one and only Son."*

John 1:14 NLT

> *"I, Jesus...I am both the source of David and the Heir to His*
> *throne. I am the bright morning star."*

Revelation 22:16 NLT

Ask Yourself:

1) What emotions does thinking about Jesus of Nazareth create in you?
2) In His day some thought Jesus was a prophet, or a rebel, or a healer, but Peter declared Jesus to be the promised Son of God. What do you think?
3) The noted writer C.S. Lewis says Jesus is either a lunatic, a liar, or who He claimed to be: the Messiah and Son of God? What's your choice, right now, today? What does facing that decision require of you?

Pray: Lord Jesus, I pray that You will come and reveal Yourself in a fresh way to me. Show me the majesty of Your Kingdom through the words of the living Bible. Draw close to me and let me have the eyes to see and ears to hear You calling me deeper into relationship. In Jesus' name. Amen.

"Left"

*"The heart of the wise inclines to the right, but the heart of the
fool to the left."*

Ecclesiastes 10:2 NIV

THE WORD FOR "left" in the Latin language is "sinister," which has come
into the English language meaning "evil." The French word for "left"
is gauche, which in English means "awkward or tactless." The English
word "left" comes from the Old English "left," meaning weak.

There are about twenty-five unfavorable references to the word
"left" in scripture. Probably the most recognized is from Chapter 25
of Matthew where Jesus speaks of the sheep on His right and the
goats on His left. The sheep are ushered into the Kingdom of Heaven
while the goats are rejected, cursed, and cast into everlasting fire
with the devil and his angels. Obviously, it is better to be on the right
side of God. We should desire to be seen as one of the Lord's sheep
and not a goat. Scripture declares the Christ is the Good Shepherd
and we are the sheep. We know that sheep have the reputation of
being vulnerable and not very bright, but why are they right with
God? And why are goats seen on the left or the wrong side of God?
Here is another example from scripture where goats are symbolized
as being bad.

*"My anger is kindled against the shepherds, and I will punish
the male goats; For the LORD of hosts has visited His flock, the*

house of Judah, And will make them like His majestic horse in battle."

Zechariah 10:3 NASB

So what is it about goats which cause God to use them in such a negative light? Goats are capricious. They are impulsive and unpredictable, devious and contrary. When they are grazing, it is not unusual to see several with their heads through a fence, straining to reach the grass that is always greener on the other side! Folklore says that goats have slit eyes to enable them to see around corners where the grazing is better. If they are not poking their heads through fences, they may be standing on their hind legs, stretching for those tender leaves just out of reach. Goats are never content with what they have. They are experts in opening gates and squeezing through small gaps because they hate to be confined. Fences that will handle sheep, cattle, and horses will not hold goats. They will work tirelessly to spring themselves from any situation they deem inhibiting. Consequently, goats are not very good followers. The herding instinct is weak in goats. They prefer leading, or being left to their own accord. Meat packers use this instinct in sheep and goats to their advantage. They will train an old goat, appropriately called a "Judas," to lead sheep to the pens for slaughter. A well-trained Judas will lead group after group of sheep to the slaughter all day long, while they go unharmed.

Goats also possess a stubborn streak. Try to grab a goat by the horns and lead it a certain direction. One can push and pull and tug, but no matter what, the goat will resist. Let go of the goat and it will eventually trot off happily any direction they want to go. Goats are intelligent and playful, but impulsive, unpredictable, and devious. Left to their own instincts, impulses, and curiosities they can put themselves in danger. They can eat "food" like tin cans which are indigestible, and head butt strangers that cause them fear. They can wander from the safety of their pasture, and lead others into slaughter.

What if these same traits were found in a Christian? What would we call a Christian who is unpredictable? Or one who thinks he is above it all? Or one who independently does his own thing? What would we call a Christian who always wants to dominate and has trouble functioning in a group? One who does not want to be led. Many of us probably have some goat-like characteristics. Many of us might be on the left side of what God may want for our lives, and struggling with "goat like" rebellion.

It is interesting that our nation's media seems to speak of the country being politically divided between the "Left" and the "Right." The Left has been associated with liberalism and the Right has been identified with conservatism. The Right has been criticized for standing on the mandates of God's Laws, Commandments, and insisting on uncompromised Biblical principles. The Left esteems itself on progressive thought, humanitarian ideas, and global, universal theology, with no absolutes.

"There is a way that seems right to a man, but its end is the way to death."

Proverbs 16:25 ESV

"Trust in the Lord with all your heart and lean not on your own understanding; in all your ways submit to Him, and He will make your paths straight."

Proverbs 3:5-6 NIV

Christians must love God first, and then love and care for their neighbors. They should not pursue after things of this world as their first love. We must learn to hear and follow the voice of our Good Shepherd. I pray that all of us would consider carefully the Good Shepherd's voice, to move rightly forward as humble sheep; avoiding the inner voice of "Judas"… our "goat nature"…so we don't turn left away from the plans

God has for our lives, our families, and our nation. May the Lord bless you, and may you always *"incline to the right,"* His right ways.

Ask Yourself:

1) What does it mean to hear the Shepherd's voice?
2) How can you prepare to hear the Shepherd's voice?
3) How are you like a sheep?
4) How are you like a goat?
5) What should you do when a Christian friend is acting like a goat?
6) Think of a time when you acted like a goat when God was trying to direct your life? What happened? What would you do differently this time?

Pray: Lord God, I want to follow you with my whole heart. I admit I have often insisted on getting my own way. I don't want to live like that anymore! I want what You want for me, Lord. Please come and be my Good Shepherd. Lead me, feed me, shelter me....fill me with the peace of letting You be in control of my life. In the name of the Good Shepherd.... Jesus....Amen!

"Lost"

---

*"Seek His will in all you do, and He will show you which path
to take."*

Proverbs 3:6 NLT

LOST? LOOK NORTH. Navigators for years have used certain tools in their travels to help direct them in their journeys. A telescope, the stars, a sextant, a map, and a compass are the trusted companions of every savvy sailor. Eagle scouts even learn to magnetize a piece of metal while using corks or leaves ballasted in water to create a makeshift compass when they are lost in the wilderness. The first step when using these tools is often to find north, specifically true north.

Unfortunately, a sextant, map, compass and finding true north seem like useless instruments when trying to navigate life and relationships... or are they?

*"The heavens declare the glory of God; the skies proclaim the
work of His hands. Day after day they pour forth speech; night
after night they reveal knowledge. They have no speech, they
use no words; no sound is heard from them. Yet their voice goes
out into all the earth, their words to the ends of the world..."*

Psalm 19:1-4 NIV

Did you know that all of creation points toward God? Scripture says,

"Ever since the creation of the world His eternal power
and divine nature, invisible though they are, have been
understood and seen through the things He has made.
So they are without excuse."

Romans 1:20 BSB

I find it so interesting that even earth's polar axis is tilted north, towards *true* north, or the truth. Jesus calls Himself the way and the truth, and, in another scripture, the door.

The Hubble space telescope reveals that Polaris, the North Star, which is the fixed star in the sky about which the entire northern hemisphere appears to rotate, is not just one star but actually a cluster of three stars. Polaris is nearly true north, and a plumb line for navigational guiding tools. NASA also states that the sky around Polaris is different than any part of the dark sky. What lies behind Polaris is undetectable. What exists behind Polaris is dark matter, or a dark expanding space which scientists have no knowledge or explanation for. Every other part of our universe has light, stars, dust, or traces of other universes, but not behind Polaris. Now, what I am about to suppose is not fact, but only conjecture, yet I think it is curious stuff.

We know that God created the heavens and the earth, and that all creation praises Him.

"Praise the Lord from the heavens, praise Him in the heights
above. Praise Him, all His angels, praise Him, all His
heavenly hosts. Praise Him, sun and moon, praise Him,
all you shining stars. Praise Him, you highest heavens and
you waters above the skies. Let them praise the name of the

Lord, for He commanded and they were created. He set them
in place for ever and ever; He gave a decree that will never
pass away."

Psalm 148:1-6 NIV

We also know that His throne is in heaven, and that it is set in the north part of heaven.

"And immediately I was in the spirit; and, behold,
a throne was set in heaven, and One sat on the throne."

Revelation 4:2 BLB

"...I will ascend to heaven and set my throne above
God's stars. I will preside on the mountain of the God,
far away in the north."

Isaiah 14:13 NLT

We also know that the Lord shrouds Himself in darkness. Look at the following scriptures.

"He holds back the face of His throne, and spreads His cloud
upon it."

Job 26:9 KJV

"Clouds and darkness are round about Him;
righteousness and judgment are the habituation of His throne."

Psalm 97:2 KJV

So, is it possible that God in His infinite design has always declared the way to truth, insight, direction, and majesty? Has nature, our poles, and our planet's rotation, even been drawn to His presence? Could the third heaven where perhaps God dwells on His throne be plainly seen in our night skies, but hidden in the darkness behind the star Polaris? Could the trilogy be reflected in the cluster of stars appearing as one? Can the Lord's greatness ever be contained, or could the ever expanding dark matter behind Polaris simply reflect His nature?

This is all just to be pondered. But the next time you feel lost…when you feel like you don't know where to go, or what to do…I suggest we take our cue from the tools of navigators all over the world. Find true north, look toward the possible direction of God's throne in the heavens, and ask Him to direct your life.

The still greater beauty is that we don't have to travel through space to visit His throne room, nor be pointed north for Him to hear our prayers. All we have to do is bow our heads and ask Him into our hearts, our minds, and our plans and He will direct our steps.

Ask Yourself:

1) Have you ever been or felt lost? Who or what helped you regain your sense of direction?
2) What does it mean to you to let Jesus be the 'true north' in your life?
3) What things in your life keep you from seeing the direction offered by God for your life? What things keep you from moving toward Him, in the best direction for your life? Talk to Him about those things today.

Pray: We thank you Father, that You have established Yourself over all things, and we rejoice in Your majesty so beautifully displayed in the heavens. Help us to turn to You when we are lost, afraid, and discouraged. Helps us to remember Your trustworthy and fixed nature to even uphold the starry night skies as they even dance around Your throne like the seraphim who cry "Holy, Holy, Holy." We bless Your name and give thanks for You and for mysteries that we can only consider. Bless us this day and keep us on the paths which will bring You glory, and take us home to be with You forever. In Jesus' name...Amen!

"Miracles"

*"Jesus replied, "What is impossible with man
is possible with God."*

Luke 18:27 NIV

DO YOU BELIEVE in miracles? Have you ever heard an account of the miraculous happening in someone's life? Do you accept it as truth or do you struggle with rational unbelief? Does your experience and logical mind interfere with the acknowledgment of something wondrous and unexplainable by human understanding? Do you know that even eyewitnesses to miracles don't always agree with what has occurred? Do you believe that God still performs miracles today? A miracle by definition is an event where the divine interrupts earthly reality and facts. A miracle is confounding and no explanation of reason can be applied to what has happened. A miracle points to God, and His love delivering grace in our earthly lives.

Have you been praying for a miracle? We don't know if Mary was praying to be the Mother of the Messiah, the destined deliverer King of Israel, but regardless, it was her God-given destiny. We should realize that even if we are not praying for miracles, the Lord can move miraculously through our lives. It seems that Mary did not doubt her miraculous fate when the angel appeared to her and told her of her future. Instead she responded in faith by just asking, "How?"

"How will this be," Mary asked the angel, "since I am a virgin?" The angel answered, "The Holy Spirit will come upon you, and the power of the Most High will overshadow you. So the Holy one to be born will be called the Son of God."

Luke 1: 34-35 NIV

The Bible is full of miracles in the Old and New Testaments, but as we reflect on miracles, especially during the Christmas season, we naturally think of the birth of Jesus. His birth was a miracle, as God stepped out of heaven and into humanity.

Do you ever wonder if God is still performing miracles today? Do you feel like miracles are something that happened only during ancient times, or does your belief and faith tell you that God is still performing miracles everyday all around us? There are those of us that have to see things with our own eyes to believe. Some of us may even be afraid to ask God for a miracle because we might be disappointed. Most of us probably have never seen a miracle, but still have the hope and faith that God has the ability and desire to do the miraculous in our lives.

"He performs wonders that cannot be fathomed, miracles that cannot be counted."

Job 5:9 NIV

As followers of Christ we have to learn to walk in faith, and not by sight.

"Trust in the Lord with all your heart; do not depend on your own understanding."

Proverbs 3:5 NLT

We have to keep a mental picture in our hearts and our minds that God hears our prayers when we call on Him. How many times have you fallen asleep at night in tearful cries of pain and worry? "Do you see me, Lord? Can you help me, Lord? Are you real, Jesus? Have you forgotten me, God? Why me, God? Can you hear me, God? Have you rejected and withdrawn from me, God? Why aren't you doing anything, Jesus?"

Are you able to say, like Job in scripture, "Though He slay me, yet will I trust Him?"

Miracles come from people's need and His loving grace. We may never understand wholly how many miracles occur in our daily lives that we are not even aware of, or why sometimes miracles don't happen even through the persistent, desperate prayers of His followers. I know that there are many of us today operating by faith and praying for a miracle in their life, or in the life of someone they love.

How do you activate the faith to believe for a miracle? First you confess your unbelief, and then ask Christ to enlarge your faith to believe for not only what He can do, but that it would be His desire and His will to divinely intervene in our lives.

"Have mercy on us and help us, if You can." "What do you mean, If I can?" Jesus asked. "Anything is possible if a person believes." The father instantly cried out, "I do believe, but help me overcome my unbelief!"

Mark 9:22-24 NLT

"And because of their unbelief, He couldn't do any miracles among them except to place His hands on a few sick people and heal them. And He was amazed at their unbelief."

Mark 6:5-6 NLT

God wants us to pray and believe Him for things that we need. He wants us to be dependent on Him; to pray and ask Him for signs, wonders, and yes, even miracles. There are times that no matter how hard we may pray and fast the Lord may let our prayers go unanswered for unknown reasons. It is in His sovereignty that we must ultimately trust during these times. I pray that you will choose to always be encouraged to pray for the miracle, hope for His promises, and then trustingly rest in His Holy Spirit.

> *"Now this is the confidence that we have in Him, that if we ask anything according to His will, He hears us. And we know that He hears us and whatever we ask, we know that we have the petitions that we have asked of Him."*

> *John 5: 14-15 NKJV*

> *"And whatever things you ask for in prayer, believing, you will receive."*

> *Matthew 21:22 NKJV*

Ask Yourself:

1) Name some of the miracles Jesus performed during His ministry on earth?
2) What miracle(s) have you experienced in your own life? In the lives of others you know personally?
3) Why is it harder to believe God for a miracle for yourself than for someone else?
4) Right now, what miracle are you seeking from God for yourself or someone else? Ask Him for it now!

Pray: Jesus, we thank You that You are never changing. Yes, You are the same today, tomorrow, and forever; and we believe that You still want to touch us and answer our prayers. Forgive us our unbelief and increase our measure of faith. We celebrate the circumstances around Your miraculous birth 2000 years ago, and the testimony of Your kingdom, Your power, and Your glory, bringing miracles into our lives today. We are so thankful for Your loving mercy and grace. You are a miraculous God! May we always testify to Your glorious acts and to be at peace for whatever Your will may be trusting in Your love, no matter what the outcome.

"You are the God who performs miracles; You display Your power among the peoples."

Psalm 77:14 NIV

"Muck"

"For we don't live for ourselves or die for ourselves."

Romans 14:7 NLT

"WHAT IS GOING on, God?" This was the fervent cry of many believers following the incredible horror and destruction of the Boston marathon terrorism incident. We witnessed the fragility of human life and the apparent total disregard of its worth. We saw the power of unity through applied focus and resources to apprehend the villains. Courage and compassion were displayed through the actions and words of bystanders of the event.

Unfortunately, not all Americans are on the same page. Mindsets are not all alike. Many people seem disinterested, uncaring, disassociated, and self-occupied. Some go about their own business as if nothing is happening in their midst, or nothing that they are willing to get involved in if does not affect them personally. They simply cannot cope or be bothered.

There is a Girl Scout song called "Bottle Caps," which has a line that sings, *"Don't dump your muck in my backyard, my backyard's full!"* Please don't download your problems this direction; I have enough of my own! Our national news and media, which seem to constantly download to the public the uncanny violence and unrest of the world, inundate our minds with the craziness of chaos. It makes no difference whether natural or manmade conflicts and disasters are reported. It all just feels like "overwhelming muck." We, as mere humans, do not have the resources, fortitude, or wisdom to solve all the problems of the world, let alone our own. Yet as believers, we know someone who does have the solutions! Scripture tells us,

"That all things are possible through Christ who strengthens me", and that, *"Nothing is impossible for God."*

Notice that the scripture says, **all**, so God means **all**. We must ask the Lord to release to us the wisdom and strategies to make a difference. He knows the necessary changes that need to happen in order to bring positive transformation to our world. What we need is a heavenly impartation of wisdom, and we need leaders, men and women, who have ears to hear and eyes to see. It should be our daily prayer: "Oh, Lord! Would You release the wisdom from heaven upon the leaders of our families, communities, churches, cities, and national governments? We need a transfer of hope, peace, love, self-control, servant-mindedness, and social consciousness." Our cry should be, "I will lovingly be my brother's keeper! How can I help personally?"

Have we forgotten the Golden Rule of doing unto others as you would have them do unto you? Many of life's situations seem hopeless, dangerous, and painfully agonizing. God has the solutions to our problems. He seems to be our only hope. There is a fear of getting personally involved in bigger problems than one's own. Instead people are resolved to pay taxes to the government or give monies to trained authorized agencies to do the work. Most of the work is hard, dirty, and emotionally draining. Helping your neighbor or a stranger can take you out of your comfort zone. Have we evolved into a society of folks unwilling to get involved, and then missed out on relishing the challenge of making a personal difference in someone else's life?

Unfortunately, many people are treading water in their own "muck" and challenging circumstances. Most people are just trying to keep their noses clean with their heads pressed down against the headwinds of economic resistance, human relativism, and a confusing "progressive" culture. Everyone needs to stop looking down, and instead look up unto the mountains from where our help comes! Join me in asking the Lord for the wisdom of James 3:17-18 for yourself and for others. It is a time to activate and release more peace makers into the land, which will produce good fruit and settle the unrest. Reach out to those who are hurting and who need a touch from the Lord. Pray for a download of wisdom and strength, and be expectant!

Pray with one another, and by God's grace we can work towards taking the "muck" to the foot of the cross together!

> *"But the wisdom that comes from Heaven is pure. That's the most important thing about it. And that's not all. It also loves peace. It thinks about others. It obeys. It is full of mercy and good fruit. It is fair. It doesn't pretend to be what it is not. Those who make peace should plant peace like a seed. If they do, it will produce a crop of right living."*

> *James 3:17-18 NIRV*

> *"So in everything, do to others what you would have them do to you, for this sums up the Law and the Prophets."*

> *Matthew 7:12 NIV*

Ask Yourself:

1) What "muck" do you want the Lord to take out of your life today?
2) Has anyone asked you to help them with a life-struggle of theirs? How did you respond?
3) Ask God to show you someone right now He wants you to help or encourage...then do it!

Pray: Lord, there is so much confusion in the world…so much wrong, so much hurt, so much pain. You know where those things are in my life, and how they hinder my walk with you. Remove that confusion from me, Lord. Open my eyes to hurt and confusion in someone else's life today, and give me the grace to approach them and the wisdom to offer Your consolation to them to help remove their load. In the Caring name of Jesus….Amen!

"Oil"

───────~───────

*"You have loved righteousness and hated lawlessness; therefore
God, your God has anointed you with the oil of gladness above
your companions."*

Hebrews 1:9 NASB

ELISHA WAS A great prophet of God. He spent his life pursuing things
of God's kingdom and His presence. He was a spiritual leader amongst
God's children. During his time of leadership there was great national
degeneracy and apostasy (a falling away from truth of the Word, or compromise with evil) much like the times in which we live. The world as
a whole was unsympathetic to God's people and to the ministry of His
Word. It was tough to be a believer and to stand for the things of God.
Many of God's people found it was often hard to even make ends meet.

Such was the case with the widow in our scripture passage.

> *The wife of a man from the company of the prophets cried out to
> Elisha, "Your servant my husband is dead, and you know that
> he revered the LORD. But now his creditor is coming to take my
> two boys as his slaves." Elisha replied to her, "How can I help
> you? Tell me, what do you have in your house?" "Your servant
> has nothing there at all," she said, "except a small jar of olive
> oil." Elisha said, "Go around and ask all your neighbors for
> empty jars. Don't ask for just a few. ⁴ Then go inside and shut*

the door behind you and your sons. Pour oil into all the jars,
and as each is filled, put it to one side." She left him and shut
the door behind her and her sons. They brought the jars to her
and she kept pouring. ⁶ When all the jars were full, she said to
her son, "Bring me another one." But he replied, "There is not
a jar left." Then the oil stopped flowing. She went and told the
man of God, and he said, "Go, sell the oil and pay your debts.
You and your sons can live on what is left."

2 Kings 4:1-7 NIV

We can relate to the widow in the passage. As we reflect on our own lives we see areas that seem to have no solution to the problem that afflicts us. It could be financial, like the widow's, or a health crisis, or emotional issues. It could even be surviving an accident or natural catastrophe. The truth is, regardless of the times in which we live and the problems we face, there is no problem or need which God cannot meet if we will simply trust and obey Him. God cares. The real issue is not the problem itself, but how will we respond or react toward trusting God? This is the crucial issue.

"But if God so arrays the grass of the field...will He not much
more do so for you, O men of little faith?"

Matthew 6:30 NASB

The widow was so destitute that the only thing she had was this tiny drop of oil. The way God generally meets our needs is to take what we have and to multiply it as we turn our lives over to Him and obey the principles of His Word. This is true of our talent, gifts, finances, or physical assets. God can't or will not put anything into full vessels without at least emptying the vessels first. As long as there were empty vessels, there was God's supply to fill them with the oil. The oil only stopped flowing when there were no more empty vessels to fill. We as earthen vessels must empty ourselves of wrong mental attitudes, priorities, pursuits, or goals, and present ourselves as vessels of God to be filled by the Word and the Spirit of God. If our lives are cluttered with bad mental attitudes, with grumbling, with selfishness, preoccupation with the things of the world and an indifference to God's kingdom, we leave no room for God to pour into our lives. God may stop the supply of oil.

> *"And this same God who takes care of me will supply all your needs from His glorious riches, which have been given to us in Christ Jesus."*

> *Philippians 4:19 NLT*

> *"...your Heavenly Father already knows your needs."*

> *Matthew 6:32 NLT*

How do we return to a place of faith, cry out to God, like the widow, wait for His instructions, and then obediently respond to His commands? How do we identify the "little bit of oil" in our lives and then surrender it to His directive? We know our own needs, but do you know that the resources are but a prayer away? Will you ask? Will you trust Him...even if the directives seem foolish or impractical? Will you allow His supernatural to invade your natural?

Ask Yourself:

1) What did the widow do that God wants us to do in times of desperation?
2) What does identifying the little bit of oil in our lives mean?
3) Why is it so hard to see the blessings instead of the difficulties in our situations? What qualities do you need in your life in order to see your blessings?

4) Think of a time when God moved in a crisis of yours in a supernatural way? How was the solution unexpected and unpredictable?

5) What resources, no matter how small, can you offer to God today? Will you?

6) What "leftover" things need to be emptied out of your life for God to fill you with His blessings?

7) Empty one "jar" of a wrong attitude or bad habit right now. Ask God to fill it with His provision.

Pray: Lord, I acknowledge that I have some clutter...some leftovers...in my life that should be emptied. You already know that I struggle with my faith to trust you to meet my needs. Lord, point me to the resource in my life, no matter how unlikely it may seem, and then help me to expect miraculous blessing and see it happen. In the name of Jesus who fed five thousand men on five loaves and two small fish....Amen!

"Pain"

---~---

*"And God shall wipe away all the tears from their
eyes; and there shall be no more death, neither sorrow,
nor crying, neither shall there be any more pain;
for the former things are passed away."*

Revelation 21:4 KJB

THERE ARE MANY forms of pain. There is the emotional pain that comes from the agony of great loss or sacrifice. There are growing pains which come from the challenges and trials in our lives, which transition us from one mindset to another. Growing pains are exceptionally difficult the older one becomes, because we tend to lose our flexibility as we age. There is spiritual pain which causes us to be separated from God, unless we receive the gift of salvation through His Son, Jesus. Spiritual pain can feel like hopelessness, abandonment, loss and ruin as one feels distant from God and from His purpose for their life. And there is also physical pain. Be it mild or intense, physical pain can color how we react to emotional, growing, and spiritual pain.

I looked into the Bible and discovered this following verse.

*"Jesus traveled throughout Galilee teaching in the synagogues,
preaching everywhere the Good News about the Kingdom. And
He healed people who had every kind of sickness and disease.
News about Him spread far beyond the borders of Galilee so
that the sick were soon coming to be healed from as far away*

as Syria. And whatever their illness and pain, or if they were possessed by demons, or were epileptics, or were paralyzed – He healed them all."

Matthew 4:23-24

I can only imagine the joy of the people who were touched by Jesus' healing ministry. The freedom, delight, celebration, and worship that would have followed would have been incredible. Imagine parents openly weeping in praise for His healing of their inflicted children. Imagine the laughter, dancing, and powerful testimony being spouted by the numerous witnesses. Jesus was amongst them! Jesus saw their suffering. Jesus was compassionate to their circumstance and He helped. *"..And whatever their illness and pain...He healed them all.* He understands suffering and has endless compassion for those hurting and who have overwhelming pain in their lives. God is willing to meet us exactly where we are in each area of pain. He is waiting for us to invite Him into our agonies of heart, mind, spirit, and physical pain. He is *Jehovah Rapha,* Lord God our Healer.

"The Spirit of the Lord is upon me, for He has anointed me to bring Good News to the poor. He has sent me to proclaim that captives will be released, that the blind will see, that the oppressed will be set free, and that the time of the Lord's favor has come."

Luke 4:18-19, Isaiah 61:1-2 NLT

"Lord, help!" they cried in their trouble, and He saved them from their distress. He sent out His word and healed them, snatching them from the door of death."

Psalm 107:19–20 NLT

"For He will rescue you from every trap and protect you from deadly disease."

Psalm 91:3 NLT

Here is the challenge: Do you believe that the words of Bible are true? Do you believe that healing from pain and suffering is available to you today? Do you believe that Jesus is willing, and only waiting for you to invite Him into all your areas of pain? Can we trust that by His Spirit, Jesus will heal us, even if He cannot be with us in His physical body? For me, it seemed that the numerous ancient witnesses to Jesus' miracles really had it made. All they had to do was be in His physical presence to receive their healing, and yet every time we bow our heads in prayer or when two or more gather in His Name, it says His presence is with us. I believe that the Bible is true. I have seen God transform the lives of friends and loved ones, but I am not satisfied. I desire to see Jesus to move in even more and greater depth of power, signs, and miracles. I ask that the Lord would stir your heart of faith to ask for the impossible…that He would come and heal you and me, and all.

"For where two or three gather in my name, there am I with them."

Matthew 18:20 NIV

"Jesus Christ is the same yesterday, today, tomorrow and forever."

Hebrews 13:8 NIV

"For nothing is impossible for God."

Luke 1:37 NLT

How many times have I fallen on my knees and asked the Lord to save and to heal? How many times has He intervened? I have seen the hand of God extend the days of a life, and I have witnessed miraculous recoveries, and I have seen men in deadly accidents survive and walk away unharmed, but it still is not enough.

I have struggled when my prayers seemed to go unanswered, when the Lord has taken loved ones home. Was my faith not enough? Why, Lord, did You not heal them? Disappointment, not peace, would fill my heart. We may never understand this side of Heaven the answers to those questions. Why do some have to endure pain? Why do some prayers seem to go unanswered no matter how much fasting and perseverance goes into prayer? His ways are higher than our ways and can sometimes go beyond our human understanding and the free will of men and women. I am choosing to not be discouraged about asking the Lord for healing, and the world's need for healing seems to be growing larger each year. Personally as I age, I find myself also a victim to the wear and tear of growing older because of the disappointment of broken relationships and dreams. I have my own daily pain which I wrestle with. Still: I choose to put my entire trust in Him. He is trustworthy. He loves me and has a plan for my life and trials are the opportunity to grow my faith; to grow more dependent on Jesus.

> *"Consider it pure joy, my brothers and sisters,[1] whenever you face trials of many kinds, because you know that the testing of your faith produces perseverance. Let perseverance finish its work so that you may be mature and complete, not lacking anything."*

James 1:2-4 NIV

I will also stand on the word of God that says Jesus still heals today. There is power in agreement in prayer. Would you pray together with me the words below? I look forward to the powerful testimony glorifying the works of God in all our lives as we walk, the walk of faith…by His grace… pain free either here or the other side of heaven.

Ask Yourself:

1) What are you crying out to God for today? What healing do you need? Body, soul, mind....finances, relationships? Ask Him to touch you right now!
2) Next, ask Him to bring someone else's need to your mind. Pray for their healing right now.
3) Will you agree to pray for them every day....and ask them to pray for you?

Pray: Father God, we come before you today seeking a touch of Your loving hand. We present to You ourselves, repenting of our unbelieving minds, and declaring the glorious promises of Your Holy word. We believe that You came to set us free and bring healing to our lives. May we receive by faith the deliverance of our flesh, the salvation of our souls, and the divine healing of our minds and bodies. May we stand in the gap, by faith, for the same healing for our friends and family members that desperately need a touch by You. Oh Lord, hear our prayers. Heal emotions, relationships, and remove disease, infirmity, infliction, and pain. Make minds clear, open eyes and ears to hear and see You. Set us free from the mindsets of this world so we can come out and worship You Lord, and declare the glory of Your Kingdom. Please hear our cry Lord and heal us all! In Jesus' name, Amen.

"Patience"

MY HUSBAND WAS preparing for an extended trip, while I was gearing up to being a single parent for the next two weeks and "holding down the fort" with our children. Happily, I support him in his travels, but there is a burden on the spouse left at home. Patience and understanding must come into play for the entire family when work, pursuit of special interests, or service to country, pulls loved ones away from their primary post. It is interesting how we may be more patient and sympathetic towards the endeavors of others if we attach redemptive value to the use of their time.

Personally, my spouse's trips allow me to joyfully make a few decisions by myself that otherwise I might have to run by my husband if he were at home. I am not advocating being manipulative behind a spouse's back, but there are certain risks to being apart; particularly leaving your family in a town that houses an adorable pet shop! We have accumulated several cute animals from this pet shop as a result of one-sided travel. I should mention there was no way to phone for spousal input due to the remoteness of the destinations, and I needed something to cuddle.

Upon returning home, my husband would reunite with us and he would graciously embrace the newest furry addition to our family! Patience was extended by both parties in this scenario; patience and understanding in the other's pursuits. Lovingly, we supported each other's decisions, and bore the consequences of those decisions together.

"We also pray that you will be strengthened with all His
glorious power so you will have all the patience and endurance
you need. May you be filled with joy."

Colossians 1:11 NLT

Patience is a virtue that is celebrated across cultural lines. Patience is clothed in wisdom, love, and kindness. Patience is also something that all of us wrestle with. It seems that the more you pray for the attribute, the more God will allow circumstances for the virtue to be developed! Just look at our freeways, highways, and byways as a science experiment to grow patience as traffic is navigated daily. School teachers, principals, coaches, nurses, and all sorts of community volunteers seem to be more naturally gifted in patience. Yet God says in scripture that one of the characteristics of His people is patience. How do we become more patient? How is patience developed in our disposition towards others?

"Since God chose you to be the holy people whom He loves, you
must clothe yourselves with tenderhearted mercy, kindness,
humility, gentleness, and patience."

Colossians 3:12 NLT

"But the Holy Spirit produces this kind of fruit in our lives:
love, joy, peace, patience, kindness, goodness, faithfulness."

Galatians 5:22 NLT

It is not by one's own power that our character is refined, but by the power of the Holy Spirit. When we, as Christians, surrender our

94

emotions and allow our lives to be transformed through the renewal of our mind by the word of God, we can indeed become new creations. We can choose to reflect love and patience because God has mercifully extended love and patience to us. Should we not extend it to others? We can allow the Holy Spirit to control our lives and lovingly exhibit obedience to what God asks us to do, which is to be patient with one another.

"Be humble and gentle. Be patient with each other, making allowance for each other's faults because of your love."

Ephesians 4:2 NLT

"The Lord's servants must not quarrel but must be kind to everyone. They must be able to teach effectively and be patient with difficult people."

2 Timothy 2:24 NLT

Let's face it: there are people in our lives that are not easy to be in relationship with. Instead of avoiding these people, what about embracing them with love and understanding? Ask the Lord to show you His perspective of their lives. Ask the Lord to see them through His eyes. It is amazing how one's heart can soften toward difficult people and situations when the circumstances are flooded by God's love, mercy, and grace. Unfortunately, sometimes it takes a great national or natural disaster to force people to work together in spite of our differences.

"Knowing God leads to self-control. Self-control leads to patient endurance, and patient endurance leads to godliness."

2 Peter 1:6 NLT

Another area of cultivating patience is learning the discipline of waiting on the Lord for direction, and developing endurance for trusting God's timing when responding to our prayers. An unanswered prayer does not mean it was not heard, nor that God will not release to you what you ask for, but is instead a timing issue. A delayed prayer can be hindered by many things, but in spite of delayed responses, we Christians must trust God's perfect timing and perfect will towards our prayers and requests. We should strive toward exhibiting patience during struggles, as well as in our normal daily lives. We can pray for God to give us the measure of patience that we need to be obedient in this task, but don't be surprised if again you find yourself in a situation to exercise it. Increased faith suspends unbelief and brings victory by His Spirit. Trust God to develop the gift of patience in your life.

"For it is not by power or by might, but by His Spirit that all things are accomplished, says the Lord of Heaven's armies."

Zachariah 4:6 NLT

Look at these other scriptures below:

"Be glad for all God is planning for you. Be patient in trouble, and always be prayerful."

Romans 12:12 TLB

"Patient endurance is what you need now, so you will continue to do God's will. Then you will receive all that He has promised."

Hebrews 10:36 NLT

Many of us have struggled with patience. Please know that even as I write this I am patiently waiting for the Lord to answer the same prayer I have been praying for twenty years. I will not give up praying. I know He hears my prayers and I know God has a plan. My prayer aligns with Heaven as I pray for the salvation of loved ones who do not know Jesus Christ as Savior, yet. I patiently pray: "God's kingdom come. His will be done," in my life and in others. I believe that with each day, week, month, and year that passes the prayers will continue to fill the censers in heaven, and in His perfect timing my loved ones will be saved. Am I impatient and wanting it to happen now? Absolutely, but I am resolute toward the goal and will not give up. Remember that patience is developed. For example, living in Los Angeles, I find that traffic really doesn't bother me. I am resigned that getting from here to there just takes more time at certain hours of the day. I have learned to accept it or to adjust my plans because of traffic. Los Angeles drivers are forced to learn to be patient on our highways or to be ever frustarated.

I want to finish with that at the end of every day, as I might curl up on the couch with a book or watching television; there sitting on my lap might be my adorable Scottish Fold cat that I got while my husband was on one of his trips. I named the cat "Patience" in fun, because who doesn't always need a little more "patience" around the house? Have I grown more patient over the years while raising a family and learning to wait on the Lord to answer prayers? I hope so, and I hope that you will be encouraged to exercise more patience in your life too.

"You, too, must be patient. Take courage, for the coming of the Lord is near."

James 5:8 NLT

Ask Yourself:

1) In what areas of your life (or with what person in your life!) do you need more patience? Pray about that right now.
2) What do you think is the difference between persistent prayer and impatient prayer?
3) Looking back over your life, what things used to cause impatience that no longer trouble you? What Holy Spirit lessons can you apply from those situations that are useful to you today?

Pray: Lord, I know I need more patience, because patience is linked with trusting You. Give me a heart full of compassion for others....and for myself....amid the struggles and difficulties of life. Open my eyes to what every situation, no matter how painful or how prolonged, is designed to teach me. Let me grow to be more like Jesus every day. It is in the Glorious and Loving name of Jesus I ask this....Amen!

"Pray"

---~*~---

"Never stop praying."

1 Thessalonians 5:17 NLT

PRAYING IS THE action, our voice is the mechanism, and our faith is the motivation to communicate with an unseen God. The book of Hebrews puts it this way: "Faith is the confidence that what we hope for will actually happen; it gives us assurance about things we cannot see." Every time we step out in faith and utter words of praise, thanksgiving, or supplication to our God; we obediently fulfill the desire of the Lord's heart. Prayer is the vehicle for us to connect with our Heavenly Father. Praying is the means of accessing the throne room of God. He desires to hear from us, for us to be in relationship with Him, to seek His will, and to be His hands here on Earth. When we pray, we are acknowledging Him as divine, sovereign, and our loving Creator. He is our protector, provider, teacher, and Savior. He has unlimited love, resources, time, and energy to move on our behalf...if we will surrender to His Lordship...if we will pray and ask Him.

"If My people, who are called by My name, will humble
themselves and pray and seek My face and turn from their
wicked ways, then I will hear from Heaven, and I will forgive
their sin and will heal their land."

2 Chronicles 7:14 NLT

"Everyone who calls on the name of the Lord will be saved"

Romans 10:13 NLT

How can I pray? What do I pray? Will God listen to my prayers? Do I have to pray out loud? My prayers don't sound like much? Will others sense my awkwardness? I've prayed before and nothing ever changed.

The statements and questions above are all too familiar to everyone in the beginning. There has to be a beginning point that we will step out in faith, and pray. But how do I approach God? If I step into a church I might get hit with lightening! Yes, it would be foolish to enter the Academy Awards dressed in the clothes we might do gardening in. Can you imagine wearing dirty jeans, a straw hat, muddy boots, and dirty gloves walking down the red carpet? In our world, it does not make sense to approach "people of power" or "places of influence" unprepared or dressed improperly, but God's Kingdom is different. The reality is that no matter how much time we might "prepare" to enter into God's Holy presence...we would fall short of His expectations. That is why He sent Jesus!!! Jesus is our covering to approach His throne. We all fall short of His glory. Scripture says,

"God sent His Son into the world not to judge the world, but to save the world through Him."

John 3:17 NLT

"I have come to call not those who think they are righteous, but those who know they are sinners and need to repent."

Luke 5:32 NLT

God says, "Come to Me. Come often, and come just as you are!" So take that first leap of faith, and bow your head and confess He is God and you are not. Thank the Lord for all that He is, and for all the blessings in your life. Take to Him the cares of your heart, and exalt Him over your affairs. Pray often and pray with the confidence that He hears you, loves you, and is so excited that you have included Him in your life!!! And come just the way you are.

"Lord, hear my prayer! Listen to my plea! Don't turn away from me in my time of distress. Bend down to listen, and answer me quickly when I call you!"

Psalm 102:1-2 NLT

"And pray in the Spirit on all occasions with all kinds of prayers and requests. With this in mind, be alert and always keep on praying for all the Lord's people."

Ephesians 6:18 NIV

"And we pray this in order that you may live a life worthy of the Lord and may please Him in every way: bearing fruit in every good work, growing in the knowledge of God."

Colossians 1:10 NIV

"With this in mind, we constantly pray for you, that our God may count you worthy of His calling, and that by His power He may fulfill every good purpose of yours and every act prompted by your faith."

2 Thessalonians 1:11 NIV

Ask Yourself:

1) When do you pray? How often? For what answers? Can you pray only in special places or times, or anywhere, at all times?
2) When does God want you to pray? Do you have to work to make Him hear you? If His Word instructs us to "pray without ceasing," why don't we?
3) What do you want to talk to God about right now? What's stopping you?

Pray: Lord, right now, just as I am, I want to approach You. I thank You that I am Your own, much-loved child. I thank You that You have promised to always hear when I call out to You. At this moment, here's what's most on my heart,_____. Lord, thank you for the faith to expect that You both hear and answer, and for the grace to know Your answer is perfect in every way; that You always want the best for me. I love You, Lord! In Jesus' name….Amen!

"Push"

"Pray without ceasing."

1 Thessalonians 5:17 ESV

I CONFESS THAT I have been called pushy, bossy, hardheaded, stubborn, tenacious, and a woman of persistent determination at times. Most of the time the people calling me these names are not observers, but instead are people groups that I am trying to lead, organize, or light a fire under. I am, at heart and will always be, a cheerleader. "Push them back, Push them back, way back!" I also know that there is a delicate balance between cheering others on and being too aggressive. I want us to look at scripture and see if there is a time to push, and a time when we should pray first and allow the Holy Spirit to do the "pressing in" with our friends.

There is a story in the Bible when friends of a paralyzed man would not take "no" for an answer. They were motivated to go against the grain and open themselves to public criticism. The companions had carried their crippled friend to see Jesus preaching at a home in a Jewish village. The house was overcrowded and no one would allow them to enter. The companions, desperate for a touch from Jesus for their comrade, climbed onto the roof, tore open the tiling, lowered their friend down through the ceiling on a stretcher, and laid him at Jesus' feet.

"Some men came carrying a paralyzed man on a sleeping mat.
They tried to push through the crowd to Jesus, but it was too great."

Luke 5:18 TLB

103

Jesus pronounced to the witnesses in the room that,

> *"Seeing their faith, Jesus said to the man, Young man, your*
> *sins are forgiven....Stand up, pick up your mat, and go home!"*

> *Luke 5:20-24 NLV*

I argue that sometimes friends can see and hope by faith for something that is beyond our own grasp or vision. I believe that having faith in the unseen and being pushy can actually benefit others at times, as well as bring glory to God. It was the belief system of the friends that Jesus was a healer that led to their tenacious behavior.

We can do the same today when we rigorously urge our friends to enter the presence of Jesus through church services, prayer groups, worship music, conversations, and reading the Bible. There is a delicate balance in moving in the Spirit's timing, but sometimes He will cause us to "push" even if it is uncomfortable or unpopular. Now short of physically forcing our friends, throwing them into a car, and then taking them to a Christian gathering (which is way too pushy!) we have the option to talk to God first. One way to know whether it is appropriate or not to push is to look at the Bible. Scripture says,

> *"Then He said to me, "This is what the LORD says to*
> *Zerubbabel: It is not by force nor by strength, but by my Spirit,*
> *says the LORD of Heaven's Armies."*

> *Zechariah 4:6 NLT*

> *"Be anxious for nothing, but in everything by prayer and*
> *supplication, with thanksgiving, let your requests be made*
> *known to God."*

> *Philippians 4:6 ESV*

You see: it is important to pray; to talk to God about our friends before we talk to our friends about God. In fact, scripture says to be pushy *in prayer*. One is to pray without ceasing. We are supposed to keep on knocking on heaven's door until He responds. In other words, *P-U-S-H* "pray until something happens". Praying will bring healing, revelation, salvation, and justice to our lives and others.

"Only by Your power can we push back our enemies;
only in Your name can we trample our foes."

Psalm 44:5 NLT

May I say that being pushy is not a very admired characteristic, but looking back I can think of the English teacher who pushed me to do better in my writing, a coach who pushed for excellence in dance, and my mother who pushed me to practice the piano, study for good grades, and to brush my teeth. All of the above had the best of intentions for my well-being, and all of the above I would consider pushy. Thank God for the drill sergeant who trains our soldiers and pushes their very limits of strength, and for the men who push our first responders to be trained for emergencies. Remember that the next time someone is pushy with you; it just might be for your own benefit and enrichment. They might be trying to bring you before the "King" for blessing in an unconventional way. But if you want to be successful as a "pusher," it is always more acceptable and victorious to push in prayer first, before you get bossy. How is the Holy Spirit pushing you as you read this devotional? Is He pushing you to come deeper into relationship with Him? Remember God has a plan and purpose for our lives. So whether you are being pushed, or you are a pusher, be at peace, knowing that God works all things together for good for those who love Him.

So, now go PUSH "Pray Until Something Happens" according to His good will and purposes!

Ask Yourself:

1) Is anyone 'pushing' you right now? What about? Is it toward God's will for your life or away from it? If it's towards God, why are you resisting?

2) Are you trying to 'push' someone for their own good? If so, have you 'pushed' in prayer first? What do you need to change about either your attitude or your approach?

3) Does the word PUSH have more meaning for you now than before? Explain and think of at least two examples where you can apply it in your life.

Pray: Lord God, there are people I love whose needs I recognize that can only be helped by You. Right now I'm thinking of................., and I bring ....before You at this moment. I ask not only for You to intervene in their lives, but also to give me wisdom and compassion. Show me the best, most grace-filled ways I can be of encouragement and help. In the name of Jesus who meets every need.....Amen!

"Rest"

"Come to me, all you who are weary and burdened,
and I will give you rest"

Matthew 11:28 NIV

I HAD COME to a place in my life that I was so weary from my daily routine and commitments that I felt like a used tube of toothpaste; not a smidge of toothpaste left in me, and no way to refill the contents. I was utterly exhausted. My emotions were spent and I found myself weepy. I questioned the choices in my life that led me to this place of exhaustion. Had I not been doing what I am called to do? I had labored for my family, the church, my friends, and lofty causes. I had loved and lavished others with bouts of hospitality and outreach. It was fun, creative, exciting, worthy, and hard work. I had been praying and ministering to others in need and in desperate times. Had I not been on the right path? Had I not been with the Lord in all that I was doing? Why had I ended up here? I was emotionally and physically undone, and I couldn't blame it all on hormones.

"Once Eleazar (a mighty warrior) and David stood together
against the Philistines when the entire Israelite army had fled.
Eleazar killed Philistines until his hand was too tired to lift his
sword, and the Lord gave him a great victory that day. The rest
of the army did not return until it was time to collect the plunder."

2 Samuel 23:9-10 NLT

I can relate to Eleazar. He fought against the enemy and did what needed to be done. The Lord gave him favor and Eleazar was victorious, but exhausted. Then the rest of the army collected the plunder, or what was accomplished by Eleazar's hard labor. As a mother, a friend, a partner in ministry, there are times when we feel like we do all this work for others, and yes, it is a valuable use of our energy to see those impacted by our efforts, but gosh, why does it seem that they always get the blessing (plunder) and all we get is exhaustion (too tired to lift our sword)? But aha! It is Eleazar that is named in the scripture, while all the others are nameless. They are referred to as "the rest". You see the Lord sees all that you do in sacrifice for others. He sees the late hours of helping your children with school work or nursing them through sickness...the kindness toward strangers...the phone calls and house calls to those who need encouragement...the times when you step aside to allow coworkers to be praised for your efforts...the extra hours of work put into generating more income...the personal sacrifice of exercise and social time to meet the needs of community or family commitments...and the battling you do on your knees in prayer. Life can make us tired and weary. Are you tired? Are you looking for a way to refuel? God has the "perfect plan" for restoration and rest in the midst of our lives. We just have to learn to follow the plan, and I had forgotten to do just that.

"Come to Me, all you who are weary and burdened, and I will give you rest"

Matthew 11:28 NIV

"The Lord is the everlasting God, the Creator of all the earth. He never grows weak or weary. No one can measure the depths of His understanding. He gives power to the weak and strength to the powerless. Even youths will become weak and tired, and young

men will fall in exhaustion, but those who trust in the Lord will
find new strength. They will soar high on wings like eagles. They
will run and not grow weary. They will walk and not faint."

Isaiah 40:28-31 NLT

I had tried restoring myself with massages, girlfriend time, recreation time, movies, vacations, shopping, etc... and none of the above was giving me rest. It was relaxing and fun, but it was not the rest which is sustaining. It was not God's rest.

"Then, because so many people were coming and going that
they did not even have a chance to eat, He said to them, "Come
with Me by yourselves to a quiet place and get some rest."

Mark 6:31 NIV

It was this last verse which finally awakened the truth in my spirit. "Come with me by yourself to a quiet place and get some rest." It was so simple. *Spend time with Jesus in prayer and solitude. Read your Bible and worship your Creator.* It won't cost you anything except your time. Anyone can do it. I needed to get quiet, and find a place where I could meet with my God. So, I did just that. I committed to the discipline of making the quiet time in the morning to read the Bible and meet with the Lord. We talked and He ministered to my weary soul. He encouraged me through His Word and gave me the strength and the peace which was lacking in my life. I listened to worship music which ministered to my heart and gave me new hope and fresh vision. He took my cares and worries, and gave me a different brighter perspective for the future. I learned to stop looking to others, things, or techniques to bring me rest. I found my rest in relationship with Him. I needed to "Be still and know that He is God."

I challenge us all to learn to be still. Are you willing to bring your burdens, sorrows, struggles, restless nights, worries, fears, and cares to Jesus? He has a great economy for exchange!

*"For I have given rest to the weary and joy to the
sorrowing. At this I woke up and looked around.
My sleep had been very sweet."*

Jeremiah 31:25-26 NLT

His ways are higher than ours, and if we continue to lean upon our own understanding we will miss the opportunity to enter into His rest, and even "sweet sleep." I urge you to come into the quiet place where God is calling you, so you can enter into His rest. I did, and I got to watch Him miraculously "refill a used tube of toothpaste," metaphorically that is! I found that true rest can only come from Him.

*"But you will soon cross the Jordan River and live in the land
the Lord your God is giving you. When He gives you rest from
all your enemies and you're living safely in the land..,"*

Deuteronomy 12:10 NLT

Ask Yourself:

1) Is there a particular part of this devotional that you relate to? Why?
2) Why is it important to know God is cheering you on through the labors of your life?
3) What are God's promises reflected through scripture in this devotional?
4) What are some ways women try to relax? How about you? Do they have value? How long do they last?

5) Think of a time when you were successful at entering into God's rest? When and how did it happen?

6) If you are weary—physically, emotionally, spiritually—what is the course God prescribes in scripture for your recovery? What do you want God to do for you today?

7) Do you have a regular time to 'recharge your batteries' with prayer and Bible reading?

8) Who do you know with whom you can share this message of God's comfort, peace and rest? Do it today!

Pray: Lord, I thank You that You are concerned about my weariness. I thank You that Jesus experienced all the same exhaustion and 'used-up-ness' I face. Take me to that place of divine peace and rest that only comes from spending time alone with You. Free me from any guilt or anxiety about leaving 'things' undone. Restore in me the joy of my salvation, and let me joyfully share this wonderful discovery with all whom You bring into my life. In the Life-Affirming, Joy-Giving name of Jesus....Amen!

"Savior"

"Today in the town of David a Savior has been born to you;
He is the Messiah, the Lord."

Luke 2:11 NIV

MILLIONS OF PEOPLE around the world celebrate the birth of Jesus through the pageantry and celebration of Christmas. The story of the star, the shepherds, the wise men, and the family traveling to Bethlehem is retold dozens of times during the Holiday season. Christmas day culminates with families and friends gathering together and exchanging gifts. Companies host parties and give out year-end bonuses, and school children sing songs during holiday performances in honor of the season. Retailers and churches will both deck their halls and encourage visitors to "Give generously, in the Spirit of love!"

Many of us will reflect on past holiday disappointments and the pressures of today. We have a tendency to analyze the depression of our economy, the growth of our waistlines, the demands of our commitments, the school finals to prepare for, and our own personal expectations of what "Christmas should be like." Also, with the decline of civility and mass shootings happening in society, it can seem like chaos reigns and that the possibility of "World Peace" has become just a beauty pageant cliché. The good news today, as it was nearly two thousand years ago, is that God had a plan from the beginning. "Today in the town of David a Savior has been born to you; He is Christ the Lord."

Man has always needed and will always need a Savior. Historically, man left to his own accord will expire. Empires of sophisticated men have come and gone. Conquerors, men of knowledge, men of fortune, and entire societies have all disappeared. They are taken out by natural disasters, wars, and the unknown. We can only speculate from the artifacts and ruins that are left behind to what became of their civilizations. On the other hand, societies that are founded on the belief system of Judeo-Christian values have prospered and still remain today.

From the beginning, God had the plan to send a Savior to the world. The question, now as always, remains: will people be able to recognize or receive Him. We can see God's plan in the following prophecies from scripture about the promised Savior; some written a couple thousand years before the birth of Jesus.

Virgin Birth

"Therefore the LORD Himself will give you a sign: Behold, a virgin will be with child and bear a Son, and she will call His name Immanuel."

Isaiah 7:14 ESV

Bethlehem

"But as for you, Bethlehem Ephrathah,, too little to be among the clans of Judah, from you One will go forth for Me to be Ruler in Israel. His goings forth are from long ago, from the days of eternity."

Micah 5:2 ESV

Shepherds

"Let the nomads of the desert bow before Him; and His enemies lick the dust."

Psalm 72:9 NASB

Wisemen

"Let the kings of Tarshish and of the islands bring presents; The kings of Sheba and Seba offer gifts... So may He live; and may the gold of Sheba be given to Him; And let them pray for Him continually; Let them bless Him all day long."

Psalm 72:10-15 NASB

"And nations shall come to Your light, and kings to the brightness of Your rising."

Isaiah 60:3 ESV

But there's also this:

The Cross

"Who has believed our message and to whom has the arm of the LORD been revealed? He grew up before Him like a tender shoot, and like a root out of dry ground. He had no beauty or majesty to attract us to Him, nothing in His appearance that we should desire Him. He was despised and rejected by men, a Man of sorrows, and familiar with suffering. Like one from

whom men hide their faces He was despised, and we esteemed Him not. Surely He took up our infirmities and carried our sorrows, yet we considered Him stricken by God, smitten by Him, and afflicted. But He was pierced for our transgressions, He was crushed for our iniquities; the punishment that brought us peace was upon Him, and by His wounds we are healed. We all, like sheep, have gone astray, each of us has turned to his own way; and the LORD has laid on Him the iniquity of us all. He was oppressed and afflicted, yet He did not open His mouth; He was led like a lamb to the slaughter, and as a sheep before her shearers is silent, so He did not open His mouth. For He was cut off from the land of the living; for the transgression of My people He was stricken... because He poured out His life unto death, and was numbered with the transgressors. For He bore the sin of many..."

Isaiah 53:1-12 NIV

Yes, our world has many wonderful things to offer us: the beauty of creation, family, friends, and the ability to appreciate good things. The problem with mankind is that our sustainability without divine guidance or faith leads to selfishness and relativity. Emotions like forgiveness and sacrifice are not highly valued unless there is an abundance of good will, resources, and peacefulness. Just watch a disaster movie and see how quickly civility breaks down and self-preservation mechanisms kick in during dire situations. People can be good, loving, and moral, but by what standards are those attributes measured? Humanism at best serves itself first; believing that man can save himself.

Those who look to the miraculous promises of God know it's all about Jesus. We can look toward a Savior in a chaotic world and trust Him to impact our own personal existence.

*"But now, this is what the LORD says-- He who
created you ..."Fear not, for I have redeemed you; I
have summoned you by name; You are mine. When you
pass through the waters, I will be with you; and when
you pass through the rivers, they will not sweep over you.
When you walk through the fire, you will not be burned; the
flames will not set you ablaze. For I am the LORD, your
God, the Holy One of Israel, your Savior... Since you are
precious and honored in My sight, and because I love you...
Do not be afraid, for I am with you ...everyone who is called
by My name, whom I created for My glory, whom I formed
and made. "You are My witnesses," declares the LORD,
"and My servant whom I have chosen, so that you may know
and believe Me and understand that I am He. Before Me no
god was formed, nor will there be one after Me. I, even I, am
the LORD, and apart from Me there is no Savior."*

Isaiah 43:1-11 NIV

Remember that God has a plan, and that you are part of it. It was the crazy, amazing plan of God stepping out of heaven in the form of child, born to a virgin, in the region of Judea, to be raised with Jewish traditions, and to go to the cross as the plan of redemption to reconcile us back to a Holy God.

A Savior was born for *you.*

*"And we have seen and testify that the Father has sent His Son
to be the Savior of the world."*

1 John 4:14 NIV

Ask Yourself:

1) What does the word 'Savior' mean to you? Do you feel the need for one? Have you asked Jesus to be your Savior? If not, stop right now and do so!

2) Since God planned to send His Son to be your personal Savior before you were ever even born, do you think you can trust Him with the rest of your life?

3) What things in your life: present situation and future needs....do you want to turn over to a loving God right now? Tell Him about them!

Pray: Lord, I believe that Jesus is not only the Savior of the world, I believe He is my personal Savior! I want to live in the faith and trust of that certain knowledge, and I want to care enough and be courageous enough to share that blessed hope with everyone I meet. In the name of Jesus, the Savior of the world....Amen!

"Scales"

JUST THE IDEA of "scales" can cause dread to rise up into the mind of any normally peaceful woman, particularly if they have to step onto one in public. I personally had a hard time while I was weighed in on a regular basis during pregnancy. The nurse would always "tch-tch" to me saying, "You know that every pound after seventeen, is just plain weight gain and not baby." Ugh! I would have to weigh in for cheerleading in college in front of our coach to see if we were staying in shape and staying at our ideal weight for those tiny uniforms. Oh, the dreaded scale.

Perhaps a personalized scripture verse should have be written for me:

*"Oh, the dread of being weighed on scales has caused me to be
heavy-hearted in the spirit, like carrying an extra 10 pound
bucket of sand from the seashore around my neck; the heaviness
and gloom of it all. That is why I speak so emotionally."*

Lamentations of Wendy

Just kidding, but no one in their right mind wants part of their private life, even their weight, to come under the scrutiny of others. We fear we will not "measure up" to the expectations of those we love and those in authority over us.

One of the most famous images of scales is the symbol of the blindfolded Lady Justice holding a pair of scales. She is the symbol of our judicial system. She represents truth, equality, and non-prejudicial judgment; honest scales. Our worldly system relies on this justice structure to measure our motives and actions. Courts, judges, and juries will observe cases and individuals and pass calculated judgments based on one's outward conduct, testimony and evidence. Only by grace do some of us never have to spend time in a court room and face these kinds of scales during our life time, but the truth is one day we will all stand before another heavenly Judge. Our Heavenly Father will look at our inward lives and measure our hearts. The question is, are you ready to stand before Him?

The good news is that as believers, and because of what Jesus did on the cross when He paid the price for our disobedience and non-perfectness, we don't have to worry about being judged. None of us will ever "measure up" to God's perfect standard, but, *it doesn't matter* if we have given our hearts to Jesus.

I pondered the question: what possibly could weigh more, a pound of my good actions, or a pound of my evil actions on the scales of life? Of course a pound is a pound, and this is not to be mistaken as a question of value between which has more power, influence, or worth...it is instead an introspective question to measure your own life's actions against God's holy standards. When searching the scriptures for an answer this is what I found about how God looks at us and the stuff in all our lives.

"No one is good not even one...For all have sinned, all fall short of God's glorious standard."

Romans 3:23 NLT

"From the greatest to the lowliest-all are nothing in His sight.
If you weigh them on the scales they are lighter than a puff
of air."

Psalm 62:9 NLT

"Yes, an ounce of foolishness can outweigh a pound of wisdom
and honor."

Ecclesiastes 10:1 NLT

God sees both the bad *and* good in our lives as falling short of His "holy" standard. But again, there is AMAZING news! When you receive Jesus Christ as your Lord and Savior, and ask for forgiveness for the imperfections in your life, and then seek His will, you then have received His promise of salvation, and the only successful way to stand up to the scales of holy judgment. It is the gift of mercy and grace that allows Father God to look and measure us through "Christ's standard." God sees only perfection because of His Son's sacrifice.

"Do not be afraid, for I have ransomed you. I have called you
by name; you are Mine. When you go through deep waters and
great trouble, I will be with you. When you go through rivers
of difficulty, you will not drown!...For I am the Lord, your
God, the Holy One of Israel, your Savior... You are honored,
and I love you.... I -yes, I alone-am the One who blots out your
sins for My own sake and will never think of them again."

Isaiah 43:1-25 NLT

"He will keep you strong right up to the end,
and He will keep you free from all blame on the great day
when our Lord Jesus Christ returns."

1 Corinthians 1:8 NLT

Yes, the Lord has a scale and indeed one day the whole world will be measured by Him.

"When the Lamb broke the third seal, I heard the third
living being say, "Come!" And I looked up and saw a
black horse, and its rider was holding a pair of scales
in his hand."

Revelation 6:5 NLT

Scales are also a representation of "balance." As women, we have to learn to balance and prioritize the many roles we play in our families and community. We are the women in the workplace, the church, the schools, the home, the highways, the beaches, the parks, the libraries, the gyms, and the marketplace. We balance the roles of mother, daughter, sister, wife, grandmother, step-mom, daughter-in-law, mother-in-law, boss, interpreter, peacemaker, bargain finder, accountant, chauffeur, stylist, housekeeper, teacher, artist, nurse, dog walker, etc... with our best effort. It is exhausting, exhilarating, rewarding, frustrating, necessary, and accepted. But we often forget to consider how the Lord measures the way we spend our time. He uses a different scale, a different priority system, when He considers the many activities in our lives. He wants us to find "balance" in our physical and spiritual lives, as well as "salvation" and the freedom it brings from His judgement scale.

"But seek ye first the Kingdom of God and all His Righteousness and all things will be added unto you."

Matthew 6:33 BLB

Martha was worrying over the big dinner she was preparing. She came to Jesus and said, "Lord doesn't it seem unfair to you that my sister just sits here while I do all the work? Tell her to come and help me." But the Lord said to her,

"My dear Martha, you are so upset over all these details! There is really only one thing worth being concerned about. Mary has discovered it-and I won't take it away from her."

Luke 10:40-42 NLT

All the many "good" things a woman does can't ever measure up to the "best" thing we can do, which is pursuing God. He is the King of Kings, and as His children, we are princesses first. Remember that of all the hats you wear, your tiara is the most important. You are Kingdom royalty. Wear your tiara and walk in the decorum, privilege, and the authority that comes with it. Don't hide your tiara under another hat, wear it on top. Your heavenly Father is awesome and wants to reveal Himself to you in a fresh way, every day. His marvelous attributes are endless. Become a God chaser, and make seeking Him, His scales, and His Kingdom a priority.

"Who else has held the oceans in His hand? Who has measured off the heavens with His fingers? Who else knows the weight of the earth or has weighed out the mountains and the hills on a scale? Who is able to advise the Spirit of the Lord? Does He

*need instruction about what is good? No, for all the nations of
the world are but a drop in the bucket. They are nothing more
than dust on the scales."*

Isaiah 40:12-15 NLT

Ask Yourself:

1) In what way(s) do you feel you've fallen short on God's measuring scale?
2) Do you know and believe that He loves you just as you are, just where you are, and just who you are?
3) What doubts and fears about yourself, what misplaced priorities, keep your focus on God from being all it should/could be? Throw those things down right now! Do you feel the weight lifted off your shoulders?

Pray: Lord, I pray today that any hindrance that stands my way of fully seeing Jesus will be bound and set aside by the power of the Holy Spirit. I ask that my eyes are opened to the path of salvation, freedom, and victory. I want to receive the blessed assuredness of spending eternity in Heaven and possess no fear of judgement, measure, or scales. I desire to find balance as I take my rightful place as a princess in God's heavenly Kingdom, and pursue after Him, wearing my tiara, with all my heart, my mind, my strength, and all my soul. In the name of Jesus, Who is all love and compassion...Amen.

*"...No eye has seen, no ear has heard and no mind has
imagined what God prepared for those who love Him."*

1 Corinthians 2:9 NLT

"Secret"

"For everything that is hidden or secret will eventually be brought to light and made plain to all."

Luke 8:17 NLT

IMAGINE THAT YOU are standing outside the courts of heaven before entering the Lord's throne room on the day of reckoning. You stand in front of doorways and gates which everyone must walk through; much like the entrances and passage ways of our airports, in order to stand before God. The ancient temple in Jerusalem gives us a picture of what the entrances to the heavenly temple might be like. There will be an outer court where anyone is given the opportunity to walk through. Jesus says, "I am the door," and that He came for all. Does Earth represent the outer temple today? The invitation to God's presence is extended to all to come and gather inside this first outer court of the temple. Yet like an airport lobby, within that first entrance a decision and commitment has to be made. Will you purchase a ticket to a specific destination and get on a plane, or turn and choose to exit the terminal? Please note that I am not saying you can buy a ticket into heaven...salvation is a gift and given by grace alone by our loving God. Choices and preparations will be needed to be made in order to be given access to the next succeeding gateways within the airport terminal. The gates we must pass through will require identification and proper screening as the traveler moves deeper into the airport's corridors, terminal lobbies, and gateway entrances to the planes. As a Christian, we will also be challenged by the Holy Spirit to become self-reflective as we are convicted, sanctified, and transformed in our personal journey with our Savior. Will you step out of the Narthex, the back row of the church, and move towards the highest altar of His love? The cost is surrender and obedience to the Father's will. Are you willing to deal with the hidden and secret things?

Before I go any further I want the reader to know that there is no condemnation in Christ Jesus. I pray that this devotional will bring reflection, revelation, conviction, and freedom. Jesus says that the truth will set you free, and I believe that when hidden things, which bring destruction, are brought into the light they become powerless. Christ can literally *save us* from ourselves. God through His word can deliver us by exposing the deceitful lies and unhealthy practices in our lives. For example, once while flying to the Galapagos islands; a flight attendant all of a sudden was walking through the aisles spraying the passengers with an insecticide. All of the passengers were fumigated whether we liked it or not, whether or not we actually had dangerous unseen hosts on our being. Protests were ignored as the attendant induced us with the irritating mist in order to preserve the sanctity of the wildlife of the region we were traveling to. I have no idea what contaminate they might have been trying to remove, but nevertheless, I arrived bug free in Galapagos. Those in authority over the region had established a protocol for anyone who will ever be permitted to enter the Galapagos. One day each of us will leave this planet and begin a journey to eternity. We will proceed toward a final destination. Scripture declares that one day all will stand in the presence of a Holy God, and some will be granted permission to enter the heavenly kingdom, while others will not be granted access. The Lord gives us His words through the Bible to help, guide, prepare, or fumigate us, in anticipation for that arrival date in Heaven. We must ask the Lord the questions, "What unseen, hidden, or secret things need fumigating in my life that I may not be aware of?" "What are the practices in my life that You are calling me to abandon or to surrender?

"Where are You lovingly trying to bring truth, cleansing, and freedom for my life?"

"But I, the LORD, search all hearts and examine secret motives. I give all people their due rewards, according to what their actions deserve."

Jeremiah 17:10 NLT

"Search me, O God, and know my heart! Try me and know my thoughts! And see if there be any grievous way in me, and lead me in the way everlasting!"

Psalm 139:23-24 ESV

After a traveler has purchased a ticket, checked his luggage, received their seat assignment and boarding ticket, they must next pass through a security check. A conveyor belt, x-ray machine, and a screening process must be tolerated by everyone in order to gain access to the next set of gates. Departure and ultimate destination cannot happen without going through this process. The contents of one's bags, purses, pockets, and even inner workings of one's body are placed before those in authority to be scrutinized. Each traveler waits with anticipation for the security guard to murmur that desired command, "Proceed!", as they stand in the x-ray machine; hoping not to have to endure an intrusive physical pat down or bag search.

I believe the Lord wants us to prepare for a heavenly security gate while we are still here on Earth. Lovingly, God encourages each of us to examine ourselves through His eyes and by the truth of scripture. Are you ready to see yourself x-rayed through the light of His Holy Word? Imagine as you might stand at Heaven's security gate and screening machine. Firstly, you place on the conveyor belt all the ways the world may judge you.

Your clothing, your physical identification described on your passport or driver's license, the money in your wallet, objects of your trade or workplace, and forms of entertainment you travel with slide into a bucket and then pass through the machine for scrutiny. Do these things reflect your interests and character? What would God say when He examines these things through His lens? What else could be found out about your character on your telephone? Who are you spending time with? What is your language like? What photos stand as evidence toward lifestyle choices on your phone? Next as all material belongings are set aside it is your turn to be physically evaluated. As you step onto the platform to receive the full body scan the Lord draws near, He is really paying attention. He will not judge you as the world judges you, instead God is interested in what is going on in the inside. What will the scan reveal about your heart and mind? What can stay hidden in secret from God?

"Stop judging by mere appearances, but instead judge correctly."

John 7:24 NIV

"You have set our iniquities before You, our secret sins in the light of Your presence."

Psalm 90:8 NIV

Have you invited Jesus into your heart? Will His presence be seen by the eyes of God in you? Have you invited the Lord into your heart and mind, and asked Him to purge you of the unseen "pests", like un-forgiveness, hatred, envy, vanity, addiction, hopelessness, selfishness, and pride that might inhabit there? The Lord is willing and capable of removing the contamination of the world through His "Holy pesticide combination spray" of love, forgiveness, and gift of salvation. The act of repentance, receiving Jesus, and life transformation happens only by the leading of

His Holy Spirit. It is the only way one is able to properly prepare to stand before God at Heaven's gate.

I have always told my children there are no good secrets. Never confuse a secret with a surprise. Surprises are only hidden until an appointed joyful time of revelation, and to the delight of the surprised recipient. When secrets are revealed they usually only bring grief and destruction. Believers have the ability to expose the hidden things in our lives that we are not proud through prayer. We seek the redeeming power of a forgiving God and we can seek the further support of other trustworthy believers to pray for freedom from the secret things. Praying with someone about a secret can bring such relief. Prayer brings freedom from condemnation of sin. The enemy will lose his suffocating grip of persecution over your mind, which feeds on the ability to make you feel lousy, sneaky, hypocritical, deceitful, and powerless. Oppositely, the Lord's love, mercy, and grace are extended to us in powerful abundance, and overwhelming covers any mistake or wrongful action that we need for reconciliation. Redemption is given to all who repent; not that this is a hall pass for habitual anti- Biblical living, but it covers all sin. The Lord can see the intentions of our hearts, bodies, souls, and minds, so He also clearly knows true repentance.

The time is coming when everything that is covered up will be revealed, and all that is secret will be made known to all.

Luke 12:2 NLT

"The day will surely come when God, by Jesus Christ, will judge everyone's secret life. This is my message."

Romans 2:16 NLT

My prayer would be that everyone would enter the courts of Heaven with an upgraded first class ticket to eternity. I pray that as we examine ourselves through the Word of God, we become convicted and motivated to walk in grateful obedience. I hope that on that Day of Judgment, when we stand at that final portal from this world into another, that we will find ourselves prepared, secret free, and delight while hearing the words of Heaven's gatekeeper proclaim, "Proceed! My good and faithful servant!"

Ask Yourself:

1) How deep into a relationship with God have you gone? Are you casual acquaintances, good friends, life-long partners....? What prevents you from having a deeper relationship with Him?
2) If prayer and daily Bible reading help you know God better, what portion of each day will you set aside for Him alone?
3) When will you spend time with God today? For how long? Doing what? Don't be afraid that it isn't enough.....just beginning is the key!

Pray: Lord, I want to enter the courts of Heaven with an upgraded first class ticket to eternity. I pray that You will seek the secret places of my heart and mind and show me what I need to remove from my life before I arrive before Your presence. Give to me the power and the strength to overcome the world through the power of Your Holy Spirit. I pray I will learn to let go of the things of this world and fix my eyes on Heaven instead! I ask for Your guidance and blessing until we meet at Heaven's gate. In the name of He Who Was, and Is, and Is to Come; Jesus....Amen!

"Shake"

*"The LORD reigns, let the nations tremble; He sits enthroned
between the cherubim, let the earth shake."*

Job 9:6 NLT

"SHAKE, RATTLE, AND roll!" is playing on my car radio as I cruise down Pacific Coast Highway. How fitting, I think, since there had just been a 6.0 earthquake in Napa Valley, California. Being born and raised in California, I have experienced enough earthquakes that I cannot honestly tell you how many I have felt or remember. The earth shakes a lot in California. You only remember the big ones. The San Andreas Fault line goes through the center of the state, and is originally named after a lake near the bay area. Saint Andreas, the Catholic believer, known for his valor and ability to overcome. Andreas means warrior in German. A fault generally means something wrong, amiss, weakness, a fracture or broken. So a literal interpretation of the fault's name could be "a valiant warring overcomer of mistakes." Boy, do we need some of that in California right now! The people in California often carry a pioneering spirit, but perhaps they have been relying too much on their own strength to overcome, and therefore they have failed? Perhaps it is a time for Californians and all people to put their whole trust back into God, and ask Him for help. God is willing to be our champion, and only He can make all the broken things right.

"And we know that in all things God works for the good
of those who love Him, who have been called according to
His purpose."

Romans 8:28 NIV

I want to believe as the tectonic plates of our state's territory clash against one another that the Lord uses this rumbling and shaking to get our attention. People have absolutely no control over earthquakes. We can control how we react to them, but minimizing or maximizing the violence of the shaking is beyond man's abilities. Experiencing an earthquake can be humbling and nerve rattling.

I believe that earthquakes are a time to remember our own insignificance to an all-powerful God and Creator. I believe the Lord can use earthquakes to shake us up, wake us up and get our attention re-focused to remember Him.

"For this is what the LORD Almighty says: In just a little while
I will again shake the heavens and the earth. I will shake the
oceans and the dry land, too."

Haggai 2:6 NLT

"The LORD reigns, let the nations tremble; He sits enthroned
between the cherubim, let the earth shake."

Psalm 99:1 NIV

The Hebrew word for shake is *"naar"*. It means to loose, overthrow, shake free, or shake off. Another primitive root of the word is the idea of the rustling of, or shaking of a mane, which usually precedes a lion roaring. We see in scripture that shaking, rumbling, and roaring accompany the Lord's presence too.

"At this my heart pounds and leaps from its place. Listen! Listen to the roar of His voice, to the rumbling that comes from His mouth. He unleashes His lightning beneath the whole heaven and sends it to the ends of the earth. After that comes the sound of His roar; He thunders with His majestic voice. When His voice resounds, He holds nothing back."

Job 37:1-4 NIV

"Your thunder roared from the whirlwind; the lightning lit up the world! The earth trembled and shook."

Psalm 77:18 NLT

And while we're on the subject of roaring, let's explore that a little further. What is really interesting about a lion's roar is **why** he roars. Experts have decided that lions roar for three reasons: One, they roar to establish territory. Two, they roar to demonstrate power. Lastly, they roar to call strays home. God, as our own Lion of Judah, also establishes territory, power, and reclaiming of strays through His voice roaring in the scriptures.

"The Lord's voice will roar from Zion and thunder from Jerusalem, and the heavens and the earth will shake. But the Lord will be a refuge for His people, a strong fortress for the people of Israel."

Joel 3:16 NLT (Territory and Power)

They will follow the LORD; He will roar like a lion. When He roars, His children will come trembling from the west."

Hosea 11:10 NIV (Calling Strays)

Interestingly, it should be noted that lions tend to roar right before dawn. Although many earthquakes also come during the early hours of the morning, the greater imagery is looking at the Lord as our Lion of Judah. Are we nearing dawn? Can you sense the Lion of Judah shaking His mane? Could the Lord be trying to get our attention with signs on the earth like the ground trembling, songs being sung by Mercy Me called "Shake," Taylor Swift's "Shake it Off," and the shaking of governments and nations? Is it a time when we should come into the understanding that the shaking precedes the roar?

I believe that it is a season to allow the "shaking" to motivate us to get free from what hinders our relationship and intimacy with God. We should cry out to Him in praise for His majesty and power. It is a time to place our steadfast trust in the Creator of the heavens and the earth for help and answers. One must surrender all control to the One who is in control, and He promises to deliver you in times of trouble. The Lion is shaking His mane, but will you be prepared for when He roars? Give Jesus your heart, mind, spirit, strength, soul, and walk in His "unshakeable love" forever and ever. We praise God for His steadfast character, and stand confident that He will awaken us to right relationship with Him, for His purposes, and His glory..." Shake, rattle, and roll"!

"Sacrifice thank offerings to God, fulfill your vows to the Most High, and call on Me in the day of trouble; I will deliver you, and you will honor Me."

Psalm 50:14-15 NIV

Ask Yourself:

1) Have you felt an earthquake how did it make you feel? How may earthquakes focus our attention on God?
2) Have you heard a lion roar? How did that make you feel? When you know that Jesus is described as 'the Lion of the Tribe of Judah," what does that make you think?
3) If you commit your life to God are you afraid of what He might require of you? What must you be convinced of to eliminate that fear?

Pray: Lord, sometimes events in this life seem like roaring in my ears! Sometimes nothing I have trusted and believed in will hold still....everything seems to be shaking! Lord, remind me that You are completely, totally and constantly reliable, trustworthy and protective of me. Do shake loose anything and everything that hinders me from having the closest possible relationship with You. In the name of the Lion of the tribe of Judah....Jesus....Amen!

"Silent"

---◡---

"A time to tear and a time to mend, a time to be silent and a time to speak."

Ecclesiastes 3:7 NIV

I FIND IT interesting that at the time of the shooting at Sandy Hook Elementary school in Connecticut, people around the nation stopped and acknowledged the tragedy with a moment of silence. There are no words great enough, nor speaker so eloquent, that could explain to us the reason, or define the insanity of the event. Even the television show, "Survivor Final Results," stopped their proceedings of announcing their "Million Dollar Winner" for a moment of silent tribute in order to recognize that something horrible, shocking, and unexplainable had happened. Innocent children, our youngest students, were slaughtered by a madman, while once again one of our public schools became a battleground. People want to react respectfully. They want to respond to the event empathetically, and they want to identify "what has gone horribly wrong" in our society to avoid this in the future. People want answers, and experts want to analyze the steps leading to the event. How could it have been prevented? Emotions seem out of control and many wonder, "How do we get control back?" Most of us just weep. Most of us just quietly give thanks that "By the grace of God, it was not I" who lost a child or loved one on December 14, 2012. Often, when we don't have words for the shocking travesties surrounding our broken world we just remain silent. Yet, in that time of silent reflection, a believer can also turn to prayer, and cry out to God.

"I lift up my eyes to the hills-where does my help come from?
My help comes from the Lord, the Maker of Heaven and earth.
He will not let your foot slip-He who watches over you will not
slumber... The Lord will keep you from all harm- He will watch
over your life; The Lord will watch over your coming and going
both now and forevermore."

Psalm 121:1-8 NLT

It is in the silence of our thoughts that the Lord can speak to us, comfort us, and bring us a peace that goes beyond understanding. "Be still and know that I am God," says scripture. As Christians, it is our duty and privilege to pray to our sovereign God on behalf of a confused and deceived world. We can pray for comfort and resolution, for protection and revelation. We can pray for the salvation of the lost, for the healing of the afflicted, and the deliverance of those being persecuted. We often pray silently in our prayer closets and in the safety of the prayer circles of our Bible studies. We will pray persistently and furiously for the Lord to intervene to come and heal the land, but is there a time when our voices need to speak up louder than the darkness? Is there not a time when our voices should arise over the tyranny of false political correctness? Is there not a time when leaders should speak the loving inescapable truth, the absolute truth, and cry out to the masses that, "The Emperor is naked?" The truth is: *man cannot save us.* The government cannot save us. The truth is that a government and a nation not submitted to God Almighty is naked. It is exposed, and dangerously vulnerable, to evil powers that would do us harm. The only one who can save us is God. He is the only One who can protect us. It is foolish to wholly trust anyone or any other system. There is a time to speak up and tell people the Good News of God's plan. Now is the time to tell people about Jesus Christ.

"One night the Lord spoke to Paul in a vision: "Do not be afraid; keep on speaking, do not be silent."

Acts 18:9 NIV

"Contend, O Lord, with those who contend with me; fight against those who fight against me. Take up shield and buckler; arise and come to my aid. Brandish spear and javelin against those who pursue me. Say to my soul, I am your salvation. "O LORD, You have seen this; be not silent. Do not be far from me, O Lord. Awake, and rise to my defense! Contend for me, my God and Lord."

Psalm 35:1-23 NLT

Christmas is the perfect time to have believers raise their voices in melodic chorus and proudly sing the wonders of God's marvelous plan. We can sing of the One who is greater than any evil, and Who loves deeper than any man. We can sing of His mighty power, His wisdom, mercy, and grace as we stroll our streets, neighborhoods and shopping centers. People can be comforted by a verse within the Christmas carol, "Away in the Manger," as we look toward trying to understand the tragedy of Sandy Hook.

Be near me, Lord Jesus,
I ask Thee to stay
Close by me forever
And love me I pray.
Bless all the dear children
In Thy tender care
And take us to heaven
To live with Thee there.

Now is the time to sing loudly a song of salvation into the void of the silence. The silence of the moment is sacred and an appointed opportunity in time for the church. We can sing the words of hope and redemption. We need to lift our voices for those who no longer have a voice, or the ability to sing. As during Christmas it is a time to sing "Silent Night."

Silent night, holy night!
All is calm, All is bright
Round yon virgin, mother and Child
Holy Infant so tender and mild,
Sleep in heavenly peace,
Sleep in heavenly peace.
Silent night, holy night!
Shepherds quake at the sight!
Glories stream from heaven afar;
Heavenly hosts sing Al-le-lu-ia!
Christ the Savior is born!
Christ the Savior is born!

Silent night, holy night!
Wondrous star, lend thy light!
With the angels let us sing
Alleluia to our King!
Christ the Savior is here,
Jesus the Savior is here!

Silent night, Holy night!
Son of God, love's pure light
Radiant beams from Thy holy face,
With the dawn of redeeming grace,
Jesus Lord at thy birth;
Jesus Lord at thy birth.

He is the hope for a desperate, dying world. He is the light to illuminate great darkness. He is the only remedy for fear and despair.

Ask Yourself:

1) Does the phrase, "Silent Night, Holy Night," feel different to you than it did before? Why?
2) Do you find the time to silence your warring thoughts, worries and busy-ness and just be in God's presence? When? Try it right now.
3) In that intentional silence, what did you hear God saying to you? Even if it was only, "I love you," and "Let's get to know each other better," it's a start!

Pray: Lord God, I want to know You better. I want Your comfort and Your peace. Please help me commit my way to You, with the resolve to be alone with You every day. Give me a voice of hope to pierce the clamor of the world, and a vision of Your holiness amid the evil that I see all around. Lord, make me an instrument of Your peace. In the All-Comforting name of the Babe in the manger....Jesus...Amen!

"Sorrow"

"My soul is weary with sorrow; strengthen me according to Your word"

Psalm 119: 28 NIV

How CAN ONE explain the loss of innocence more clearly except to compare it to the agony and emptiness of sorrow? The feelings of remorse for what once was, and will now never be again. Sorrow is when one must grieve the love, the hope, or the peace stolen from them, the abandonment, and the betrayal. How can one assess the depth of pain of a broken heart filled with sorrow, when what was treasured is now lost? Can that treasure be measured in worth? I believe the answer is yes, if the love and peace of a contented heart is seen as priceless in value. It truly is what everyone is searching for in life, whether they know it or not. When Jesus took all our sorrows on the cross, He understood these same emotions and the painful agony of relational bankruptcy.

"For sure He took on Himself our troubles and carried our sorrows. Yet we thought of Him as being punished and hurt by God, and made to suffer"

Isaiah 53:4 NLT

Jesus was separated from the Father when He cried out, "Abba, Abba, why have You forsaken me? Jesus felt alone. Jesus felt scared, Jesus felt the sorrow of perfect love and peace being removed from Him at that moment on the cross, yet He cried, *"Not My will, but Your will be done."* The depth of the love of the Father was the sacrifice of His Son. The depth of the love of the Son was obedience, and the sacrifice of experiencing not only the sorrow of man, but the sorrow of being separated from God.

Sorrow is a human experience. It is desperate longing for what could have been or was. It can be initiated by the end of a relationship, a death of a loved one, a career, or a dream unfulfilled. It is being forced to say goodbye to someone or something. Sorrow can catch you completely unprepared emotionally and completely out of control of the situation. Sorrow deals with the separation of peace from our psyches. Peace and love are stolen from our body, mind, and spirit. It is a time of grieving and reflection. Sorrow must be felt. Unreleased from our hearts, sorrow will cause us to fall short of moving forward with our lives. One can get stuck in the grieving process, which will cause us to get stuck in a loop of regret and frustration.

> *"You turned my wailing into dancing; You removed*
> *my sackcloth and clothed me with joy, that my heart*
> *may sing Your praises and not be silent. Lord my God,*
> *I will praise You forever"*
>
> *Psalm 30:11 NIV*

We must take our sorrow to the cross like Jesus, and we too can cry out to God, "Father, why?" We can grow and learn to trust and rest in the understanding that God is in charge, *"not my will, but Your will be done."* What we might see as chaos could really be a part of the Lord's plans for us, as *"His ways are higher than our ways,"* and *"God's way is perfect."* Sorrow will bring change. Wet tears can water the garden of one's future if we allow God into the process, healing the wounds of mourning and sorrow.

It is foolish to think that one will ever escape feeling this emotion. Sorrow is a human condition. It is intrinsically connected to love. To love deeply is to risk sorrow sometime in the future. Why cannot we just love or dream, and not experience the emotions of loss and sorrow when they seemingly depart from us? Why do bad things have to happen? Why cannot unconditional love and peace exist in all relationships and in the entire world? Oh Lord, I pray that you would take my sorrow. I pray that I could exchange it for the joy and strength of the Lord. I pray that You God will heal the brokenhearted and remove the sorrow, and bring *"the promise of joy in the morning"* instead of *"ashes and terror by night."*

"A time to weep and a time to laugh, a time to mourn and a
time to dance"

Ecclesiastes 3:4 NIV

We may never understand the *whys* of sorrow, but I don't think we are to rest in the land of shame, blame, could of, should of, or what ifs. We must fix our eyes on Jesus and move forward toward Him. His Word says, *"I will never abandon you, and I am with you always until the end of time."* It is God's promise. We must walk by faith and not by sight. We must put all our trust in Jesus, and take our sorrow to Him. Of course, much easier said. Below are the words from my heart to God as I pray may His will, not mine be done.

Who am I to say?
That I don't like the ways of dying and living
Who am I to say?
To question His purpose while the world keeps on spinning
Who am I to say?
It's not right, it's not fair, and it doesn't make sense
Who am I to say?
Empty and void from this circumstance
Make me strong, make me sure
Fill me up, make me true
Take my heart, take my pain

Undone, black and blue
Abba Father, help me, to trust You.

-WENDY

"Blessed are those who mourn, for they will be comforted"

Matthew 5:4 NIV

Ask Yourself:

1) What is the deepest sorrow you have in your life? Have you given it to God? Do You believe He is great enough…and cares enough…to comfort you? Can you believe to trust God to turn sorrow into joy?
2) Are you able to move toward Jesus in spite of past sorrow, anger, bitterness or guilt?
3) If Jesus experiences sorrow and grief, what does that say to you? What do you want a compassionate and merciful God to do for you today? Tell Him right now!

Pray: Lord, take our hearts and hold them in Your merciful hand and heal the wounds of lost love, abandonment, and rejection. Help us to look forward and to not look back. Help us to recognize and trust that instead of grieving and focusing on what has been lost, we can cling to the promise that You, Lord, *"Will work all things together for good for those who love You."* In the name of Jesus Who knows all our sorrows from His own experience….Amen!

"Success"

―~―

*"In everything he did he had great success, because the Lord
was with him."*

1 Samuel 18:14 NIV

How DOES THE Lord measure success? How does the world measure success? How do you measure success? These three questions have been nagging at me as I have been trying to prayerfully guide and encourage my adult children and husband into their God-given destinies. Each of us has one life to live, one life to express love, compassion, and to explore the unlimited potentials of each of our own unique journeys. The older I become, the more I find I need more grace toward my family in allowing them to seek their own paths. Instead of following my ideas, expectations, and common sensibilities, I have had to adjust to letting go of my dreams for their lives and watch them pursue their own dreams. I ask my loved ones constantly, "Have you prayed about it?" whenever they seek my advice regarding choices as they chase after their dreams. Unconventional paths and pioneering outlooks seem to be the norm in our house right now. I am amazed as one door opens and another door shuts in each one's life. I, being the "follow the rules, self-reliant girl," have had to learn to be more and more flexible in my conclusions, and spend a lot more time in prayer seeking divine guidance. I am learning to trust the Lord and grow deeper in my faith than ever before. "How do you know that you are on the right track?" "What does success look like?" The secret to success is very simple. It is just one thing. It is abiding in Christ Jesus.

"Be strong and very courageous. Be careful to obey all the instructions Moses gave you. Do not deviate from them, turning either to the right or to the left. Then you will be successful in everything you do."

Joshua 1:17 NIV

"Remember the Lord your God. He is the One who gives you power to be successful, in order to fulfill the covenant He confirmed to your ancestors with an oath."

Deuteronomy 8:18 NLT

"Trust in the Lord with all your heart and lean not on your own understanding; in all your ways submit to Him and He will make your paths straight."

Proverbs 3:5-6 ESV

I encourage all of us to press into His presence and follow the leading of the Holy Spirit in all our decisions. Today's society is littered with social land mines of compromise and temptations. We must be led by the word of God to be successful. The Lord draws near to those who will humble themselves and seek His face, His heart, and His wisdom. Do not allow man's expectations, priorities, and accolades to steal your time, monies, and energies. We are in a time of "His ways are higher than our ways" in seeking a life successfully led.

What does success look like from a heavenly perspective? I share with you my own experience: It is dwelling in peace that goes beyond human understanding. Success is knowing who I am in Christ, and how much my heavenly Father loves me. It is the confidence that my shortcomings are forgiven and that He is with me always. One can even experience "Kingdom success" while enduring "earthly failure". It is the peaceful knowledge that although you may experience great loss; you can maintain your principles, integrity and trust in the God. Steadfast faith in adversity is success in the Lord's economy.

I know that all my success in life is through His goodness working through me and that His gracious hand has been on every project and relationship where I have invited Him in. Our failings come from not remembering God's instruction to us. "Loving the Lord with all our heart, soul, strength, and mind," and abiding in Him, will grant us success; not the success the world can measure through merits, awards, finances, and titles, but knowing that our talents and resources successfully served the King and His Kingdom. I tell my friends that a Christian life is like a trip in the old days to Disneyland where you were given a book of tickets to all the rides in the park. One's goal was to use up all the tickets before you left the park by the end of the day. Metaphorically the Lord has given each of us a book of tickets, gifts, resources, and talents. Some tickets seem more prized than others in the book. These valued tickets, when submitted to the leading of the Holy Spirit, can get you on the most amazing ride of your life! My goal is to not leave this life with unused tickets for His Kingdom in my pocket! I pray that you too will trust the Lord like never before, pressing in through prayer, seeking His wisdom, letting go of earthly expectations, while having the courage of walking in complete confidence of His leading. May the Lord be with you. May you always acknowledge His blessings and grant you success!

"May the Lord bless and keep you; May the Lord make His face shine on you and be gracious to you; May the Lord show you His favor, and give you peace."

Numbers 6:23-26 NLT

Ask Yourself:

1) In the past, what things meant "success" to you?
2) What does success mean to you now? How do you want success to be defined in your life from now on?
3) Are you holding any special 'E ticket' which you haven't used yet? What's stopping you?
4) What barriers exist between you and the kind of supernatural success you desire? Ask God to remove those barriers right now!

Pray: Lord God, right now, and from now on, I want my definition of success for my life to match Yours! I don't want to wander to the left or the right out of Your plan for me, because by staying in the center of Your will I know I will have heavenly triumph. Bless me with that clarity of vision and purpose right now. In the name of Jesus, Who 'set His face like flint' in order to keep the Father's will....Amen!

"Time"

—⁓—

*"There is a time for everything, and a season for every activity
under the heavens."*

Ecclesiastes 3:1 NIV

"I'M LATE, I'm late, I'm late!" cried the White Rabbit as he ran across the
country landscape while grasping a pocket watch, before quickly disap-
pearing down into the ground. The Rabbit seemed to be swallowed by
the blackness of the deep, dark hole he entered.

I would love to name that black pit of darkness "expectations, commitments, should do-s, great ideas, new projects, family obligations,
dreams to be fulfilled, busyness, have to-s, social engagements, celebra-
tions, deadlines, legal requirements, work duties, and even recreational
exercise." All of us can get pulled into deep holes of time-sucking activities which tug at our precious daily allotment. Each day brings the same
amount of minutes. We are each given twenty four hours with each rotation of the earth, but why does it seem that some people have greater
success in using their time? Or do they really? How do you use your time?
Are you a good steward? How do you waste your time? What do you wish
you had more time for in your life? Theoretically, we all have the same
amount of time; some of us just need to adjust our priorities. Through
prayer and the Word of God we can align ourselves with Heaven. We can
pray that God will adjust our lives to reflect His priorities for the time
and season we are in. That black hole can change from being a place of
chaos and anxiety into a place of peace and repose. The mistake people

make is thinking that doing it all, and doing it now, will bring happiness and fulfillment. Instead of always being in a hurry to cram everything into one day and losing the joy of the journey, we need to slow down, exhale, and prioritize. We need to trust God that if he calls us to "Be Still" or "Pour Out" that our responses should be "Yes, Lord!", and then obediently surrender to His Spirit. What would the world be like if every believer asked God, "How may I serve you today?" And then responded in accord to His leading?

> *"God has made everything beautiful for its own*
> *time He has planted eternity in the human heart,*
> *but even so people cannot see the whole scope of*
> *God's work from beginning to end."*

Ecclesiastes 3:11 NLT

> *"I have observed something else in this world of ours.*
> *The fastest runner doesn't always win the race, and the*
> *strongest warrior doesn't always win the battle. The wise*
> *are often poor, and the skillful are not necessarily wealthy.*
> *And those who are educated don't always lead successful*
> *lives. It is all decided by chance, by being at the right*
> *place at the right time."*

Ecclesiastes 9:11 NLT

It is so important to be at the right place at the right time. Opportunity and blessing come from being in the will of God. We need to listen to His calling and not our consciences, self-wills, or worldly pressures. How blessed is the person who takes time from their day to step out of their own schedule and are willing to sacrifice their agendas to "be there" for a friend? How blessed is the individual who will forego that workout or manicure appointment to take a meal to someone grieving or home ridden? Each of us has a limited time here on the planet Earth. Some have fewer days than others. Scripture says that our days are numbered, and that there is an appointed day for which we are born and an appointed day that we die. We must learn to use our time wisely and honor our Lord with the time that we have been given. We must be ready to give an account of how we have used our time.

"Moreover, no man knows when his hour will come."

Ecclesiastes 9:12 NIV

"You also must be ready all the time. For the Son of Man will come when least expected."

Matthew 24:44 NLT

It is so important to understand the significance of how we spend our limited time here and how it will affect our eternity. *"All who call on the name of the Lord will be saved"* Romans 10:13, but each believer wants to arrive in Heaven where our Master says, "Well done, good and faithful servant!" We must guard our time fiercely from the world and submit it daily at the foot of the throne of God. Instead of chasing time, always striving to catch up, may we become God-chasers, forever led by His Spirit!

"May the favor of the Lord our God rest upon us; establish the work of our hands for us-yes, establish the work of our hands."

Psalm 90:17 NIV

Ask Yourself:

1) What things in your life do you spend the most time on? Be honest! How many of those have value for eternity? What is your biggest time-waster?

2) Do you ever feel you must defend the way you spend your time?

3) What would God say to you about how you spend your time?

4) How many of the things to which you devote your limited time are good for you? How many build you up? How many provide contentment?

5) How should thinking about eternity and eternal things affect how you spend your time now?

6) Whom do you wish you could spend more time with (either living now or someone deceased who was part of your life)? Why?

7) How should your daily agenda change for you to draw closer to God? What one thing will you change today?

Pray: Lord God, I recognize that I have only so many minutes in each day and a handful of days in each week. I also know that I spend too much time on things that are unprofitable...for my spirit, for my emotions, for my relationship with You and with others. Help me to truly prioritize my life with a view toward eternal values. I know, Lord, that in You lie peace and contentment, and that in scurry lies frustration. Help me to slow down long enough to focus on You and get Your clear direction for my life. In the name of He who is the Lord of the hours and the days and the weeks and the years.....forever and ever....Amen!

"Tears"

---~---

"...This is what the LORD, the God of your father David, says:
I have heard your prayer and seen your tears..."

Isaiah 38:5 NIV

DO YOU REMEMBER the climactic scene of the "The Passion of the Christ," where Jesus gives up His life on the cross? The ground shakes, the skies grow dark and ring with thunder. Next a single raindrop falls from heaven, hitting the earth, signifying the mournful tear of our Father in heaven grieving for His Son. We are moved to tears of our own.

While watching the scene in a Kodak commercial where the overwhelmed child is miraculously reunited with his beloved lost dog; the scene suddenly comes to an instrumental crescendo, and I find a single empathetic tear sliding down the side of my cheek.

People cry. It is a human quality. These days I believe that I have become quite an expert at it. I have endured the harsh, irritating tears falling from my eyes while cutting raw aromatic onions.

I have cried tears of joy and laughter, my favorite kind, as when retelling the story of the young nervous bride, me, discovering that as I removed my dress after the wedding I had not removed the stiff, dry, cleaning cardboard from the garment before putting it on. No wonder I was uncomfortable!

I have had the experience of weeping slow, deep tears while being moved by the beauty of the music being played by a symphony at Carnegie Hall. And I have cried anguished tears of great pain and loss in the emotion of losing a loved one. Did you know that God sees, records, and collects all our tears? Tearing eyes are also a part of the animal kingdom, but humans are the only ones who tear from emotions. Why would God collect and remember our tears if He did not think they were precious? It is comforting to me that He sees them as important to Him.

"You keep track of all my sorrows. You have collected all my tears in Your bottle. You have recorded each one in Your book."

Psalm 56:8 NLT

There exists three major types of human tears: basal, reflex, and psychic (triggered by emotions). Basal tears are the natural tears which lubricate and keep the eyes moist, while reflex tears are triggered by irritants to the eyes like onion fumes, which the reflex tears help wash away. Psychic tears are associated with crying and weeping due to strong human emotions from physical pain, laughter, grief, joy, or in response to beauty in art or music. All tears contain organic substances including oils, antibodies, and enzymes that are suspended in salt water. Different types of tears have distinct molecules. Psychic tears have protein-based hormones, including the neurotransmitter leucine enkephalin which is a natural painkiller released when we are stressed. It is one of the natural reasons one feels better after crying. Are we not wonderfully and fearfully made?

I have always marveled at how simple it is for some people to cry and so difficult for others. All of us have shed tears from irritants to the eyes, but crying psychic tears is different. One must be relaxed with their emotions and trust that letting go of emotional control is safe and acceptable. Is it a condition of one's heart? Is crying limited as socially appropriate only to the female sex and children? To laugh, cry, or express pain without inhibition is to be childlike and not self-conscience of one's actions impacting others. Jesus tells us in order to receive the Kingdom of Heaven we should have that same childlike trust and abandon to

Him. I want to examine the Biblical truth that there is an appropriate time to cry; that there is an importance to tears, and to cry is to be in good company! Scripture shows us that there is a time for everything under Heaven, and that the Lord hears our crying.

"...a time to weep and a time to laugh, a time to mourn and a time to dance..."

Ecclesiastes 3:4 NIV

"... This is what the LORD, the God of your father David, says: I have heard your prayer and seen your tears..."

2 Kings 20:5 NIV

"The Lord has heard my cry for help. The Lord receives my prayer."

Psalm 6:9 NIV

Jesus himself wept tears of emotions. Scripture records that Jesus wept at least two times as an adult. Once, before He called Lazarus out of his tomb, and a second time as He gazed at Jerusalem shortly before His appointment at Calvary.

"Jesus wept."

John 11:35 NIV

"Now as He drew near, He saw the city and wept over it, saying, "If you had known, even you, especially in this your day, the things that make for your peace! ...because you did not know the time of your visitation."

Luke 19:41–44 NIV

"During the days of Jesus' life on earth, He offered up prayers and petitions with loud cries and tears to the One who could save Him from death, and He was heard because of His reverent submission."

Hebrews 5:7 NIV

I like to think that our tears are like liquid prayers; that crying is a tangible expression of our hearts and emotions at times when our words fail us. I believe that letting the tears flow freely is healthy. We know that scientifically our stress in subdued by the chemical release of neurotransmitters, but by faith we know that God receives these liquid prayers and accounts for them. Jesus wept as He called Lazarus out of the grave, perhaps not only because of sympathizing with the pain and loss of Lazarus's loved ones, but also He grieved on a personal level. Jesus was witnessing a foreshadowing of His own death and resurrection. It grieved Him that He would have to physically suffer and die, and be placed in a tomb. He was overcome by His emotions. These tears or liquid prayers do have influence in heavenly places. Look at these scriptures of tearful intercession and the promises attached to them:

"My intercessor is my friend, as my eyes pour out tears to God."

Job 16:20 NIV

"Those who sow in tears will reap with songs of joy."

Psalm 126:5 ESV

"...Weeping may tarry for the night, but joy comes with the morning."

Psalm 30:5 ESV

There is a time when believers need the support, love, and liquid prayers of their friends and family. There is a time of tearful celebration of joy and a time when intense pain can cause us to cry out to God together. For those who may be crying today from personal suffering remember that there is hope in Jesus. God promises that there is joy in the future for those who mourn. I know that healing is a process, and that we can trust a God that loves us so much that He collects, records, and understands our tears. Many people find solace in crying in the shower. It is a good private place to allow your salty tears to mix with the fresh warm water, and then to let them be literally washed away. Yet remember not all the water goes down the drain. Our Lord has captured your precious tears into His heart, into His bottle, for all eternity, and understands the cost of those tears. The cost is the depth of one's love poured out for another. So go ahead and have a good cry and pray like rain, and whether it is a few raindrops or a cloudburst...the Lord is ready to receive your tears!

"I served the Lord with great humility and with tears ..."

Acts 20:19 NIV

Ask Yourself:

1) What situations make you cry? Every time or sometimes?
2) How does it make you feel to know that Jesus wept? That He felt sorrow and grief? How do you explain that and what does it mean to you?
3) How does it make you feel to know that God sees and cares about your tears? Do you have deep sorrow you want to offer to Him right now?

Pray: Lord God, I thank you that you care about the things that make me sad. I thank you that Jesus experienced every level of grief and sorrow the same as me and that He understands exactly how I'm feeling. Lord, please take my tears and make them a positive blessing. Use my sorrow to soften my heart toward the problems experienced by others. Thank you that a time is coming when You will "wipe away every tear" from our eyes. In the Matchless, caring name of Jesus who feels our grief....Amen!

"Trust"

---

*"But blessed is the one who trusts in the Lord, whose confidence
is in Him."*

Jeremiah 17:7-8 NIV

ARE YOU TRUSTWORTHY? Who do you trust? Can God be trusted? What
are the attributes of someone or something you can put your trust into?
The times we are living in seem to be ever less secure. Can we trust the
precepts and institution of marriage in a changing world? Can we trust
our churches? Can we trust our banking and financial system's honesty?
Can we be assured of the fiscal stability of homes and real estate that we
have invested in? Can we trust doctors, the medical community, or in-
surance agencies with our health care? What will the future bring? Can
we hold onto the promises of our national leaders for the future of our
families? Is their leadership dependable, consistent, and reliable? Do the
people you love say what they mean, and mean what they say? Are they
trustworthy?

I think we can all agree that measure of "trustworthiness" in a person, thing, or organization can only be defined by one's personal relationship, history, or experience with them. Everyone will have their own
unique perspective of what they find trustworthy and whom they may
trust. Do you know that God wants to trust you? He wants a personal
relationship with you. He wants you to be His friend. He wants to share
His secrets with you.

"...From everyone who has been given much, much will be demanded; and from the one who has been entrusted with much, much more will be asked."

Luke 12:48 NIV

"You have been permitted to understand the secrets of the Kingdom of Heaven, but others have not. To those who are open to My teaching, more understanding will be given, and they will have an abundance of knowledge..."

Matthew 13:11-12

God wants you to understand that even before the creation of the Heaven and the Earth that He had you on His mind. He knows your thoughts and been with you always. His love for you is steadfast and unchanging. Every time you give thanks for the blessings in life, God smiles and delights. Your faithfulness touches Him every time you bow your head in prayer and invite Him into the comings and goings of your life. Followers of Christ have learned that the more you release yourself to Him and devote your energies to His Kingdom...that the result is ability to develop a "deep personal trusting relationship" with the Creator of the Universe. He will never abandon, nor forsake you. He promises to be with you always, even until the end of time.

God the Father has given His all, through the sacrifice of His Son, Jesus, to make a way for you to enter the throne room of Heaven and to share your heart and thoughts with Him. He has bet everything that you are trustworthy of His lavish love. Will you accept His invitation of a personal relationship with Him? He is the only one completely trustworthy of your love.

"Those who know Your name will trust in You, for You, Lord, have never forsaken those who seek You."

Psalms 9:10 NIV

Ask Yourself:

1) Who do you trust? What makes them trustworthy?
2) Can you be trusted? How have you shown it?
3) Can God be trusted? How do you know? Has He shown you that He is trustworthy? What things in your life do you need to trust Him with right now? Tell Him!

Pray: Lord, in the midst of a chaotic and an ever shifting planet, who better to invest in than a Savior named "Jesus?" I know I am being called to a deeper level of understanding of how to trust God in these unsettling times. I pray that I may also be found trustworthy as You pour out Your prayer strategies, dreams, and visions upon me. May I be trusted to use those gifts and talents, and walk confidently in the gifting and visions upon me. May my faithfulness, through Your Spirit, bring healing, deliverance, beauty, compassion, and hope to a desperate world. May You continue to be magnified and glorified through my words and actions. In the Mighty name of Jesus, Who is altogether Trustworthy... Amen!

"Truth"

"Guide me in Your truth and teach me,
for You are God my Savior, and my hope is in You all day
long."

Psalms 25:5 NIV

WHAT IS TRUTH? We can offer a definition like "Truth is that which conforms to reality or fact", but this basic definition is open to personal interpretation. What is reality? What is fact? How does one's perception affect truth? Man over time has developed many theories to answer these questions according to the relativism of the culture and personal preferences, but the Bible gives us a warning to use discernment when it comes to the "revelations of men." We can be deceived of the truth. Truth is not self-contradictory. Truth is not deception.

" I am telling you this so no one will deceive you with well-
crafted arguments...See to it that no one take you captive
through philosophy and empty deception, according to the
tradition of men, according to the elementary principles of the
world, rather than according to Christ."

Colossians 2:4-8 NLT

We must be careful to not accept the false mindsets of influential men and women in this world who put their belief and trust into the systems of this world, instead of God.

165

"Do you not know that the wicked will not inherit the Kingdom of God? Do not be deceived: Neither the sexually immoral, nor idolaters, nor adulterers, nor male prostitutes, nor homosexual offenders, or thieves, or greedy people, or drunkards, or those who are abusive, or cheat people- none of these will inherit the Kingdom of God."

1 Corinthians 6:9 NLT

If we believe that absolute truths exist apart from cultural and personal preferences, then we must acknowledge that there exists a *source* of truth. For the Christian, the ultimate expression of truth is found in the person of Jesus and in the Bible. The justification is that the Bible claims to be inspired by God.

"All Scripture is God-breathed and is useful for teaching, rebuking, correcting and training in righteousness"

2 Timothy 3:16 NIV

Look what Jesus said about truth. Jesus answered,

"I am the Way and the Truth and the Life. No one comes to the Father except through Me."

John 14:6 NLT

"You are truly My disciples if you remain faithful to My teachings. And you will know the Truth, and the Truth will set you free"

John 8:31-32 NLT

Of course, most philosophers and skeptics will dismiss His claim, but for the Christian, Christ is the mainstay of hope, security, and guidance. Followers of Christ use the Word of God for their plumb line of truth. We cannot afford to compromise God's truth to what society may find reasonable, rational, or tolerant. A Christian's world-view should always be filtered by the "ultimate lens of the truth", the Bible. Jesus, who walked on water, claimed to be divine, and rose from the dead. He said He is the truth and the originator of truth. If Jesus is wrong, then we should ignore Him. But, if He is right, then the Bible is true, and we should follow Him. What will you believe about Him? What will you decide? Is the Bible true? Will you conform to the mind of Christ? Christians receive Jesus as the "truth" and follow Him by faith. The "truth" is that as a follower of Christ, one just chooses to receive by faith His unconditional love and gift of salvation. I pray that we may all become bearers of the "Love of Christ" to others, and learn to walk in truthful obedience and uncompromising love for Jesus.

> *"And you also were included in Christ when you heard*
> *the message of truth, the gospel of your salvation. When*
> *you believed, you were marked in Him with a seal,*
> *the promise Holy Spirit"*

Ephesians 1:13 NIV

Ask Yourself:

1) Jesus said He IS the truth? What do you think He meant by that? What does that statement mean to you?
2) How important is truth in dealing with God? With others? With yourself?
3) What truth about Jesus do you need more of in your life? Ask Him for it now!

Pray: Lord, I believe that Jesus is "the Way, the Truth, and the Life." I want all of that in my life. I want to live each day....each moment... in Your path for me, surrounded by and living in Your Truth, in the fullness of the abundant life you have for me. Lord, make me a person of Truth, inside and out. No deception for me, Lord. Not of me by myself, not by me of others and not of me by others. In the name of the Truth.... Jesus...Amen!

"Valentine"

"God's beloved. God's permanent residence.
Encircled by God all day long within whom God is at home."

Deuteronomy 13:12 MSG

"VALENTINE, WILL YOU be Mine?" Have you heard the softly whispered voice of the Lord speak these same words to you? Can you remember a time when you sensed the presence of His Spirit lovingly calling you into deeper relationship with Him? *Beloved you belong to Me, I have called you by name, and I have paid the ransom for your life. Will you not love Me back? Will you surrender your heart to Me? Will you allow yourself to be loved by Me completely? May I be your One and only?* When we approach the celebration of Valentine's Day each February, perhaps each of us should consider more closely this invitation from the Lord, *"Will you be Mine?"*

No greater gift has been given than the opportunity to find redemption through the grace of Christ's sacrifice. His obedience at the cross created the access to salvation for all who call on the name of the Lord, seek forgiveness, and believe in Him. You can't figure your way into heaven through wisdom and understanding, and you can't work your way into heaven by doing good things. You cannot ride into Heaven on the tailcoats or prayers of another; even if you're somehow related to Mother Theresa. Each person needs to respond individually to the invitation of grace. Each person needs to carefully consider the eternity and consequences of their answer. It is between you and God. He relentlessly pursues us, but are you listening? Are you pursuing Him?

> *"But from there you will seek the LORD your God, and you will find Him if you search for Him with all your heart and all your soul."*

> *Deuteronomy 4:29 NASB*

Scripture declares the desire of God's heart is to be the primary focus of our love. He wants a covenant relationship with us. He desires to be first in your life; that we should trust Him, obey His commandments, and allow Him to direct the paths of our lives. We must be seeking Him; actively looking for Him in order for Him to reveal Himself to us.

> *"Know therefore today, and take it to your heart, that the LORD, He is God in Heaven above and on the earth below; there is no other."*

> *Deuteronomy 4:39 NASB*

> *"Oh that they had such a heart in them, that they would fear Me and keep all My commandments always, that it may be well with them and with their sons forever!"*

> *Deuteronomy 5:29 NASV*

> *"You shall love the LORD your God with all your heart and with all your soul and with all your might."*

> *Deuteronomy 6:5 ESV*

It is interesting to point out that the human heart is an organ with four different chambers. The human heart has four compartments of empty space through which blood is pumped. It has two atria, related to the context of a "wide open area much like the outer atrium space before stepping into the sanctuary of a church"-*see Webster's dictionary*. It also has two ventricles, from the Latin word "venters" meaning *belly*. Prayers of salvation include the passage of inviting Jesus into your heart, but have you invited God into all four chambers of your heart? Have you invited God entrance to the inner chambers, and not just access to the atrium? Have you made some of the rooms of your heart off limits to His presence or purpose? Can you hear Him now speaking to you about a compartment of your heart which needs some spring cleaning? A place where maybe you are holding onto un-forgiveness, pride, or broken dreams? *"Will you be Mine...will You give me all of you?"* Will you allow Christ to come into all four chambers, and make room for His Spirit to bring amazing healing and deliverance? Will you say yes? Will you humbly allow Him to exchange the things of self and mortality for eternity and Living Water?

"Whoever believes in Me, as the Scripture has said,
that out of their bellies will flow rivers of Living water "

John 7:38 NLV

Jesus came to set the captives free, to fulfill the scriptures, to heal the broken-hearted, and to give us everlasting life. Just as the human heart takes the tired, lifeless blood and then pumps oxygen and life back into the blood, so is the transformational power of the Holy Spirit operating in the life of a believer. There are multiple blessings one receives as His Valentine. God promises to listen to us, and He strengthens, renews, and revives our hearts.

"O LORD, You have heard the desire of the humble;
You will strengthen their heart, You will incline Your ear."

Psalm 10:17 NASB

"Create in me a clean heart, O God, and renew a steadfast
spirit within me."

Psalm 51:10 NIV

"The humble have seen it and are glad; You who seek God, let
your heart revive."

Psalm 69:32 NASB

"And I will give you a new heart, and I will put a new spirit
in you. I will take out your stony, stubborn heart and give you
a tender, responsive heart."

Ezekiel 36:26 NLT

Each day of life that we have been given is a gift from God. His grace and love abounds, even if we fail to recognize it. Each day God calls us to come closer, to share our hearts and dreams with Him. Each day we have the opportunity to commune with Him through His Word and through prayer. Please do not miss the invitation every February to respond to His calling. When Jesus reveals Himself to you in that special way which is only for you, and for your understanding of who He is, I pray that you will say yes! "I will be Yours. I will be Your Valentine!" I pray that none of us will harden our hearts and close our eyes and ears to His Words and presence. Don't allow unbelief, fear, regret, or human wisdom stand in the way of your eternity. Look at these words of warning from Jesus:

"When you hear what I say, you will not understand. When you see what I do you will not comprehend. For the hearts of these people are hardened and their ears cannot hear and they have closed their eyes- so their eyes cannot see, and their ears cannot hear, and their hearts cannot understand, and they cannot turn to Me and let Me heal them."

Matthew 13:14-15 NLT

Jesus wants to bring victory to every arena of our lives, as demonstrated through the transformational physical, emotional, psychological, and spiritual healing by His Spirit. Say yes, to Jesus, and tell Him He can have all of you, and give Him back the best Valentine ever: your heart.

Ask Yourself:

1) What parts of your heart have you not allowed God to enter? Why not?
2) How do you know God loves you? How has He shown you His love?
3) How can you show your love to God today? What do you want from God's love today? Talk to Him about those things right now!

Pray: Lord God, You are All Love! You loved me while I was still an enemy of You and opposed to Your will for my life. Lord, I give You access to all my hidden chambers and innermost secrets! Clean me out, fully and completely. Let me love You, and afterwards others, with Your kind of divine, all-caring love. Give me a new understanding of what it is to love and be loved....right now, today! In the name of the One who loved me enough to die for me....Jesus....Amen!

"Worth"

*"A wife of noble character who can find? She is worth
far more than rubies."*

Proverbs 31:10 NIV

HOW MANY TIMES do women fall into the trap of measuring their self-worth according to the standards of a secular world? The world would judge us by our achievements, our beauty, our weight, our children's behavior and achievements, our pet's behavior, the husbands we've married or lack of husband that we have, our career, the cars we drive, the schools we've attended, the clothes we wear, our abilities to cook, the houses we keep, the savvy of our bargain shopping, our recycling and devotion to a "greener earth" and community service, what parties we've been invited to, the places we might vacation, and even where we might attend church. The list seems endless...we even judge the intake and consumption of food in ourselves and other women. Thoughts inundate our minds like, "Was that really a healthy choice of calories for me or her? Will anyone notice that I am only one eating the bread at the table?" "How can I possibly live up to everyone's expectations?"

Women! Relax! Although the wife of noble character from Proverbs 31 is a "superwoman" doing and being it all, do not miss the fact that there is a question mark after the statement. This gal is priceless because she does not exist. Proverbs 31 is a role model for us to strive towards, to emulate in making sure we use our gifts and care about others, but the "heart" of a woman is the true object beloved by God. Do you know how priceless you are to God? Jesus gave His very life so He could spend eternity with you. Is it not a relief that there is nothing you can do to make God value you less or more? He loves us just the way you are. He judges you only by your belief in Him. It is your faith in Him, your heart entrusted to Jesus, that He finds value in. Also, a woman of faith is just not valued here on Earth now, but for all eternity, by a loving Heavenly Father.

"These have come so that your faith-of greater worth than gold, which perishes even though refined by fire-may be proved genuine and may result in praise, glory and honor when Jesus Christ is revealed."

1 Peter 1:7 NIV

"Instead, it should be that of your inner self, the unfading beauty of a gentle and quiet spirit, which is of great worth in God's sight."

1Peter 3:4 NLV

Women, we need to let go of earthly measuring sticks, and see ourselves through God's eyes. If we let our self-worth and happiness be standardized by man and not God, we will find ourselves never being able to weather the storms or changing seasons of our lives. Yet, if our faith is steadfast, then so should be our belief and confidence that we are the "beloved children of the Most High God." The measure of our worth should be in knowing, deep in our souls, that we are loved and saved by Jesus. The peace, joy, love, self-control, perseverance, wisdom, etc..., which comes from this revelation…is the priceless confirmation of finally understanding that it is only what God thinks that truly matters. The truth is that you are unconditionally loved by Him. So I pray that you will let go of false expectation of yourself, surrender insecurities, while rebuking the lies of the enemy that rejection from men means that you are unlovable or have no worth. I pray that you experience the fullness of Christ's love in your heart. His love is of great worth and has priceless eternal value. May you see your self-worth only through His eyes, and not by what others may think of you. May you know the "value of your worth" through your relationship with Jesus, and not solely by the roles, deeds, attributes, or relationships you may have with others. Will you give Him your whole heart today and receive His love? I pray that you will. In Jesus name, Amen.

> *"And I pray that Christ will be more and more at home in your hearts as you trust in Him. May your roots go down deep into the soil of God's marvelous love. And may you have the power to understand as all God's people should, how wide, how long, how high, and how deep His love really is."*

> *Ephesians 3:17-18 NLV*

Ask Yourself:

1) By what standards have you valued yourself in the past?
2) By what standards have you valued others in the past?
3) How does God value you? How does He want you to value yourself? How does He want you to value others? How should a "God's-eye" view change the way we look at ourselves and others? Ask Him to begin that change in you right now!

Pray: Lord God, I thank You that You value me through the lens of Your Son! Thank you that when You see me, You see Jesus! Help me to see myself that same way....but don't let me stop there. Help me to see others in that same loving and compassionate way. Lord, make me an instrument of Your peace, but letting me express loving concern to all I meet. I love You, Lord, and I want everyone to know it...through my attitudes, actions and words. In the name of Him who valued me enough to die for me....Jesus....Amen!

The Last Word:
"The grace of our Lord Jesus Christ be with you all. Amen."

Revelation 22:21 KJB

About the Author

Wendy Miller is the heart, CEO, behind "All Things Wendy," www. allthingswendy.com, which was formed in order to be a platform for creative expressions in design, writing, social media, business, and Christian ministry. Wendy acknowledges the tongue in cheek play on words for her company while trying to describe her multi-tiered interests and passions. Her first passion being Jesus Christ.

For Wendy, it's all about Christ; the author, the inspiration, and architect of All Things Creative. Wendy dedicates her God given gifts and talents of creativity to bring as much impact as possible to her areas of influence. She invests her time to selected projects including interior design, authoring books (*The Little General, He Gets The Last Word, and The Shell*), and serving non-profit foundations committed to the arts and Christian evangelism. Wendy is the founder and Executive Director of the Cantinas Foundation, which exists to transform our modern day culture through opportunities where God can be magnified through the arts.

Her logo features "Wendy" under the roof of a house highlighting the cross as a symbol that Wendy acknowledges that she is able to accomplish "All Things Through

Christ" who strengthens her. She is supported by an incredible team of dedicated employees, friends, mentors, and family. Deep in the center of her heart is a love for Christian evangelism and she hopes to be a blessing to everyone who encounters anything "All Things Wendy".

Made in the USA
Las Vegas, NV
24 February 2021